Nature and Grace

Other books by the same author published by
Darton, Longman and Todd

Your God?
Open the Frontiers
Charismatic Renewal and Social Action:
A Dialogue (with Dom Helder Camara)
Renewal and the Powers of Darkness

Nature and Grace

A Vital Unity

CARDINAL LÉON-JOSEPH SUENENS

Malines Document V

Darton, Longman and Todd
London

First published in Great Britain in 1986 by
Darton, Longman and Todd Ltd
89 Lillie Road, London SW6 1UD

The English translation was made by
Olga Prendergast from the French edition

ISBN 0 232 51670 7

British Library Cataloguing in Publication Data

Suenens, Léon-Joseph
Nature and grace; a vital unity
1. Christian life—Catholic authors
I. Title
248.4′82 BX2350.2

ISBN 0–232–51670–7

Phototypeset by Input Typesetting Ltd, London SW19 8DR
Printed and bound by Anchor Brendon Ltd
Tiptree, Essex

Contents

Preface

This *Malines Document*, the fifth in the series, examines the relations between nature and grace in order to harmonize them or, more precisely, to avoid overestimating the role of nature to the detriment of grace in an adequate Christian formation.

It lays special emphasis on the danger of naturalism, which, generally speaking, is not one that threatens the Charismatic Renewal; nevertheless, I hope that it will help its readers to avoid pedagogical methods in which nature and grace are not harmoniously blended, and to restore the balance if needs be.

Besides, our time is so steeped in naturalism that it would be helpful, I believe, to make a brief analysis of the phenomenon for the use of every Christian who wishes to be, in the fullest sense, a human being and a disciple of Jesus Christ.

Some things go without saying . . . but go even better when said. There are silences which, by omission, create imbalances. 'To disregard a point is not the same thing as lying', people sometimes say in their attempt to justify a one-sided view. This may sound convincing in theory, but we are not entitled to shelve vital complementary truths, even as a temporary measure. In the same way, a doctor who cares for the human body must not overlook the psychic elements which frequently intervene in somatic disturbances.

When we are dealing with the formation or the analysis of the Christian, we must constantly bear in mind that man, who is so rich in natural gifts, is also a fragile, wounded being, and that the contribution of grace is an integral part of his healing and growth.

May Our Lady of the Incarnation and Pentecost help us to live and to make fruitful, in fellowship, all the riches in man's heart and, even more intensely, all the renewing riches of the Holy Spirit, which are in God's heart and destined for man.

+ L.J. CARDINAL SUENENS

I

Between Two Dangers

1. THE PARADOX OF THE CHRISTIAN LIFE

Many years ago I much enjoyed a book by Mgr Benson entitled *Paradoxes of Christianity*. Each chapter opened with two apparently contradictory texts from Scripture, such as the Lord's words: 'I have not come to bring peace but the sword', followed by: 'My peace I give you, a peace that no man can take away from you.' This contrast between two texts obliged the reader to be aware of the coexistence of simultaneously true, but apparently conflicting, realities: 'the coincidence of opposites', to use a philosophical term.

The same applies to the twofold respect which must govern our behaviour: respect for the requirements of human nature, allied with respect for the exigencies of grace. How can the personality and richness of man—living man whom St Irenaeus calls 'the glory of God'—live in harmony with that other man within me, who is also myself, and who must rid himself of his weakness, practise self-renunciation in order to thrive, and in short 'be and not be' simultaneously?

2. THE CHURCH BETWEEN CHARYBDIS AND SCYLLA

The Church must ceaselessly navigate between Charybdis and Scylla: between the double danger of supernaturalism and naturalism. In other words, it must steer a course between the tendency to distort the supernatural through exaggeration and the tendency to distort the place of the human by overestimating its role and its self-sufficiency. To discover the right balance between grace and nature is a daily struggle in the history of the Church and in the heart of each Christian.

To find the happy medium, we have to distance ourselves

from supernaturalism:

I have stressed this point in the previous *Malines Documents*, where I say plainly to the Renewal: do not exaggerate exorcisms, prophecies, 'resting in the Spirit', the simplistic rejection of the human sciences;

and also from naturalism:

Naturalism takes man as its starting point. It envisages him as an intact, unwounded, sinless being, whose subjective imperatives must be followed as a rule of life and self-fulfilment. In extreme cases, he is an autonomous being whose Ego dictates his every action. He is a law unto himself, despite his experience of fluctuation, doubt and questioning.

3. THE CONTRAST OF GENERATIONS

Each new Christian generation, faced with the duty of harmonizing nature with grace, is marked by the temptation to overestimate grace to the detriment of nature, or vice versa.

In the sphere of ethics and spirituality, my own generation was marked by a certain supernaturalism which did not comply with all the rightful demands of nature because it was insufficiently acquainted with the psychology of the conscious and unconscious mind. Some aspects of our moral teaching were particularly deficient in this respect, thus giving rise to narrow, rigid views, taboos, lists of sins improperly categorized as mortal, and so on. One of my first interventions at Vatican Council II was a plea that this whole area of teaching be revised.

We also suffered from an excess of individualism in our human and Christian relations. The individualistic atmosphere was hardly conducive to mutual openness, sharing or the exchange of deep feelings, even among Christians living together as a community. There was a kind of discretion, reserve and self-constraint in our relations. The deep self was accessible only to God in prayer, and to the confessor or spiritual director. Hence quite a few people suffered from psychological blocks and—as a natural reaction—when this or that method suddenly unblocked unacknowledged psychological repressions, the experience could be traumatic.

Admittedly, the situation I have just outlined deserves to be more carefully qualified; but here I am simply indicating yesterday's tendency so that we may better understand why people are going to the opposite extreme today.

Almost inevitably, when we overemphasize one aspect, we understate whatever does not support our case. Some years ago I wrote a booklet entitled *The Role of the Human in Supernatural Growth*, in which I attempted to show that, like a seed, grace needs to fall into fertile soil, cleared of weeds and rubble, in order to thrive. When the soil is unfavourable, the human person easily drifts into supernaturalism, that is to say, an artificial supernatural. I believe that, at the time, it was important to stress this danger.

4. THE NATURALISTIC REACTION

Yesterday's history helps us to understand, if not to justify, the present over-reaction. For when a society reacts too strongly, it ends up by disregarding the indispensable complementary aspect. 'I like coexisting truths', says a character of Claudel. But we always find it difficult to balance assertions which seem conflicting, whereas in reality they are complementary.

I remember that when I taught pedagogy in the seminary and used to ask my students, 'What must you know above all when you're teaching John Latin?', how delighted they were with the answer: 'Above all, you must know John.' Well, our time has repeated this so often, and brought John so prominently to the foreground, that today we must say and repeat: 'But you must also know Latin.'

5. IN SEARCH OF THE RIGHT BALANCE

The same is true of our duty to respect the exigencies of both nature and grace. I believe that in those days we had to react against supernaturalism in order to save the supernatural, but at the moment we must react against naturalism in order to safeguard the supernatural.

Here I am deliberately underlining the danger of naturalism, for the atmosphere of our time is so thoroughly steeped in it that it is useful, I believe, to point out its exaggerations in order to help every Christian who wishes to be fully human and fully a disciple of Jesus Christ. It is this fundamental conviction which has inspired me to write these pages.

What we must focus our attention on here is not the statement of this or that author, but the basic tendency underlying certain methods of introspection and analysis. If, in a particular case, the author or promoter does not recognize himself in the statement of an unacceptable doctrine, or has evolved since he wrote it, so much the better. I am reminded here of the celebrated seventeenth-century controversy between the Jansenists and their critics. The latter denounced the five Jansenist propositions drawn from the *Augustinus* of Jansenius, the famous Bishop of Ypres.

The defenders of the incriminated book said that they were quite willing to reject the propositions themselves, but they vigorously denied that they were even present in the *Augustinus*. This lesson from bygone days urges us not to become too involved in the interpretation of the authors themselves, but to react against the doctrinal implications when they are incompatible with the Christian faith.

A deeper knowledge of human psychology can be a valuable instrument of grace. But the methods themselves need to be relativized and completed. They must be studied with discretion and discernment. It is this comprehensive view that I will attempt to set out in these pages, stressing the specific requirements of the Christian faith.

II

Idolatrous Egotism and Christian Faith

We are living in a strange world where egotism has taken the place of the worship of God. Our customs have become so deeply imbued with this new idolatry that most of our contemporaries take it for granted.

1. ABSOLUTE EGOTISM IS TAKING THE PLACE OF THE ABSOLUTE

The 'I' has become the point of reference for all moral conduct. The Greek philosopher Protagoras already stated long ago that 'man is the measure of all things.' Today this has become an indisputable criterion governing the life of individuals. Everything is judged and evaluated from the standpoint of the ego and in accordance with an overriding self-centredness. Let us note in passing that 'self-centredness' is not the same as 'selfishness', which implies a moral judgement, but the two terms—and the reality underlying them—have much in common. In English a neologism 'selfism' has been forged to mark the distinction. The advantage of this vocabulary is that it allows us to remain on the phenomenal plane, at least for our present purpose.

For we really are faced with a new phenomenon. Since man has broken away from God as his vital point of reference, he has to seek another point of reference in order to motivate and justify his conduct. And self-centredness is providing him with a substitute religion, an alternative absolute.

It is not by chance that the forefathers of egotism were the forerunners of modern atheism. Feuerbach, the father of today's atheism, stated quite plainly that 'man is man's god' (*homo homini deus*). He believed that this discovery was the decisive turning-point in the history of the world. In varying degrees, traces of Feuerbach's atheism can be found in Marx (who borrowed from him the well-known phrase 'religion is the opium of the people'), Nietzsche, Huxley, Rogers and Maslow, to name but a few. They are the prophets of the new age who were to bring the world happiness once men were wholly and permanently liberated from religious alienation. But as far as this promised earthly paradise and temporal messianism are concerned, we are now poles apart from what they had hoped and predicted for mankind. There is little need to labour this point, for we have only to read the morning paper or watch television in the evening to see where we stand!

Let us take a close look at the consequences of this 'death of God' which is relentlessly leading to the death of man.

2. 'I': THE SUPREME POINT OF REFERENCE FOR GOOD AND EVIL

A preliminary question must command our attention: is the 'I' really an absolute, a basic datum? Or is it itself conditioned and relative?

These question-marks inevitably arise from the moment that the 'I' claims to be the supreme criterion of human values and conduct: if my ego is my supreme rule of life, why should I respect that life which was given to me without my prior agreement? Why should I continue to accept that life if it becomes intolerable to me? Why should I not dispose of it as and when I please, and determine its end at my own convenience? As we know, Camus saw the predicament of suicide as the key-problem of philosophy. Why, indeed, should one continue to live when there is no valid reason for living?

Furthermore, who will give my 'I' its certificate of authenticity? The very history of the promoters of that substitute religion shows that the actualization of the 'I' can lead its followers to a wide variety of positions. The 'I' of Martin Heidegger, the best-known of the Existentialist philosophers, led him to espouse Nazism for a while. The 'I' of Karl Jaspers led him to liberalism. To follow the philosophy of the ego can be as dangerous as walking on quicksand: the absolute 'I' turns out to be eminently relative.

According to the logic of the system, whatever fosters the spontaneity, sincerity and authenticity of the 'I' is called 'good', and whatever inhibits them must be 'bad'.

But what is the moral value of these ambiguous terms? Professor Rezsohazy of the University of Louvain recently wrote these pertinent lines on the subject:

> For the rising generations, the first criterion of moral action is authenticity, which means that man personally commits himself through his choices, provided that they are sincerely in accordance with what he believes he should do at a given time, independently of any abstract principle . . .
>
> Today, the most frequently used moral expressions are words like 'authenticity', 'spontaneity', 'personality', 'identity' and 'autonomy'. Well, the obvious danger is that you can murder someone 'spontaneously' or be 'authentically' unfaithful to your wife.
>
> These terms are criteria for judging *how* an action should be done, but they fail to tell us whether the action is right or wrong.
>
> This frame of mind, which is more concerned with the personal circumstances of one's behaviour than with the

intrinsic value of human actions, easily ends up by 'psychologizing' the moral problem.[1]

What creates a problem at the level of the individual equally creates one at the broader level of society as a whole, at least in the West. The rules of the democratic game are based on an addition of autonomous and supreme egos: our laws are at the mercy of the fluctuations of those egos, which are added up by computer and depend on the majority view that emerges. Any day the great collective 'I' can decree and legalize whatever suits it best.

Today our parliamentary debates on the right to abortion are opening the way to predictable future discussions on the right to suicide, the right to planned euthanasia motivated by pity, the right to go unpunished for certain crimes which, by then, will be called by new names, depending on the prevailing fashion. For there will no longer be any intrinsic reason for curbing our collective moral vagary.

3. THE 'I' AND ITS AMBIGUITIES

The 'I', promoted as the centre of man's morality and full development, is never 'chemically pure'. It must be freed of the ambiguities that surround it in order to play the sovereign role assigned to it. This raises a number of preliminary questions merely on the human plane.

First, one would like to know what innate or social factors unconsciously fashion that 'I', before it is let loose and given its credentials and sovereign power. Moreover, if 'authenticity' is determined in relation to my ego, does this mean that everything I have not chosen of my own free will is unauthentic? Why should I love my parents, who did not consult me about bringing me into the world? Let us remember how Job complained about that very situation.

Then, if man is innately good but disfigured by society, we would still need to know why society, composed of equally good individuals, manages to unleash evil social forces and fratricidal wars. Furthermore, if we acknowledge (and how can we deny patent facts?) that the 'I' is composed of several layers, often in conflict and at war with each other, who can say which is my true self, and in the name of whom or what can I choose between those rival tendencies? St Paul already spoke of the good he wished to achieve and the evil to which he was drawn: he acknowledged quite plainly that he was torn between these two conflicting aspects of the self.

The ambiguity of the ego is also revealed in the scientific sphere. Whether we are dealing with psychiatry or with psychology, in its Freudian or other forms, we are forced to the conclusion that man is a wounded being, and that the 'I' is also, to a significant degree, the plaything of the obscure forces of the unconscious: the work of identifying and harmonizing all the aspects of man's being and behaviour is unending, and science itself still has far to go in this direction. Here it will suffice to mention a few aspects which are also inherent and 'natural' in man from the outset, and which exhibit his aggressive, selfish or possessive tendencies. The child left to himself without a guide is not an ideal and spontaneously good human being.

So the 'I' is not a wholly reliable guide which, alone and unaided, leads to human happiness. Besides, nature herself is equipped with reflexes, as it were, to protect man against what denatures him and arbitrarily distorts his true finality. Let us reflect on these lines of Bergson:

> Some philosophers who have speculated on the meaning of man's life and destiny have failed to notice that nature herself has taken the trouble to give us her own teaching on the subject. She notifies us by a precise sign when we have

> reached our destination. That sign is joy. I say joy, not pleasure . . .; pleasure is but an artifice conceived by nature to ensure that life is preserved in the living being: it does not indicate the direction in which life thrusts itself . . . . Wherever there is joy, there is creation: and the richer the creation is, the deeper is the joy.

These words are a key which helps us to locate the blossoming of the 'I' in its true human depth.

1. From the review *Humanités chrétiennes*, 1982.

III

Hypertrophic Egotism

1. THE HUMANISTIC PSYCHOLOGY

Idolatrous egotism is clearly incompatible with the Christian faith, but there is a hypertrophic egotism which is even more subtle and fallacious, and equally incompatible with Christianity because of its ambiguity. The underlying causes of this danger, which is inherent in various types of psychoanalytical or psychological analyses, are manifold: a distorted vision of man, a psychology that degenerates into psychologism, a silence about essential or complementary human aspects, or again a misuse and overdose of introspection.

There is already an immense literature and a wide variety of studies on this subject. What concerns us here is above all the common traits, tendencies as such. In America, C. William Tagason, Professor at Notre Dame University (South Bend), has given us an overall view of the problem in his book *Humanistic Psychology: a Synthesis*.[1] This valuable scientific study is essentially informative, although the author occasionally brings in his own critical comments.

To my knowledge, there is no French equivalent of this encyclopaedic type of study, and one must often look for its sources in dispersed publications not always available to the general reader.

Generally speaking, it must be acknowledged that the success of humanistic psychology and its offshoots, even in Christian circles, is largely due to our own sin of omission as Christians. We possess an exceptionally rich spiritual literature, but we have not sufficiently elaborated a corresponding pedagogy, seeking to harmonize nature with grace in man's development. We have not paid enough attention to everything that helps man to know himself, to form himself, to open himself to others, to be altruistic, to share his spiritual wealth. We still have to fill the gap. I bear this in mind when, in what follows, I emphasize the deviations and defects of certain current methods.

To lay a finger on what may be rightly called the hypertrophy of the ego—a danger inherent in these methods of analysis—we must take a closer look at their aim and their ways and means of reaching it.

2. THE PRIMACY OF THE EGO

(a) *What is the aim?*

The primary and permanent aim of these methods is to help the person to take an interest in himself, to build himself up, to find himself or the best in himself: his true and authentic self. To this end, he is advised to free himself of his estrangement from others and its social conditioning, to cast off his inhibitions, and to learn to be faithful to lived reality. In the final reckoning, the aim is that each subject should discover the right to organize his life, to be responsible for it, to act in accordance with his own conscience and personal intuitions. He is told that a good relationship to and with himself can only further his relations with others and with an inner absolute which has to be discovered.

Furthermore, we learn that to reach this goal, the subject

must start from the experience of 'the positiveness of being', which refers him to an unspecified 'greater good', written without capitals for the time being, though perhaps it can subsequently take a rather vague capital letter: e.g. Justice, Conscience, God, Truth, Love.

Contrary to the personalist vision which prevails today, these theorists of the 'I' do not see the human being as 'a being-with-others', permanently constituted as such through the dialogue he establishes with his human environment. The idea of an active, constructive reciprocity is conspicuously absent.

In the circumstances, the *inner life of the individual* is given absolute priority: each person carries the truth of his being within him, and it would seem that neither his fellow men nor the structures of his society contribute anything to his personal identity. So the main function of others is to 'enable' his inner wealth to emerge.

To some extent, this philosophy reflects the liberal individualism of the nineteenth century, which was wary of social influences and made the free development of each individual its ideal.

In this light, one understands why so little importance is attached to structures. And this position is strengthened by the extraordinarily naive view that individuals thus 'liberated' are bound to have a 'contagious' effect on others, and will gradually but inevitably transform the whole social body.

From the outset it is clear that such a teaching overlooks a major achievement of the human sciences: their acknowledgement of the considerable influence and originality of structures in both the dynamics of society and the growth of persons.

(b) *How is the aim reached?*

To reach the desired goal, the subject must endeavour to lay bare his innermost being, understood as an autonomous centre which cannot be identified with reason, or the will, or freedom. In order to reach into that innermost self, like a deep-sea diver, he must manage to analyse his own inner states, described as 'sensations'.

In order to free this inner man so that he can 'stand on his own feet', the most favoured approach is the totality of the subject's sensations or 'inner states', often described in bodily terms. It is presumed that once they are acknowledged and properly analysed, the 'core' of one's being will be discovered.

The analysis of the subject's present sensations gives access, first of all, to the *I*, the person's autonomous centre and pilot. Going even deeper into the centre, one reaches being or the Ego. The analysis of sensations uncovers the positive aspects of the I–Ego.

Individual introspection is the path by which truth is attained. When it is practised in a group, assisted by a guide, this diving into oneself is often effected in an atmosphere and by means of directions which, to some extent, govern the discoveries which the subject will subsequently make. Hence the possibility that the subject is being manipulated cannot be excluded. The guide does not lay bare his own innermost being, even unconsciously, and, willingly or otherwise, he influences the members of the group. It is important to be aware of this if we want to judge the matter fairly.

The image of man which will emerge is concentric, in the manner of certain oriental wisdoms: there is a nucleus or core, 'the innermost centre of being', as indescribable, we are told, as God himself. And this is the one and only locus of truth and love. Around this centre revolve the secondary elements: the body, reason, the will. It is presumed that from the moment one reaches the innermost core, everything becomes organized and harmonious of its own accord: the body and its drives find a lasting wisdom whose fruit will be a permanent equilibrium.

3. A GLANCE AT A FEW SELF-ANALYSES

To grasp the concrete results of this type of method, assuming that it is practised from beginning to end, we have merely to note certain typical comments that are invariably made by the advocates of these self-analyses.

— 'Helping people makes me feel better.'
— 'Was I my true self today?'
— 'Now I've the courage to be wholly the master of my actions.'
— 'I can let my heart live without asking anyone's permission. I've a right to life and happiness.'
— 'An action is good in so far as it upbuilds me.'
— 'My ideal: to be myself, only myself, wholly myself, and to heal myself through analysis.'
— 'I can't live without this training which makes me happy.'
— 'To be solely oneself, not like others.'
— 'I must rely on my sensations and their fluctuations, and sail on the river of sensations.'
— 'What matters is not what I know, but what I feel.'

I shall return to these sentiments presently.

4. SELF-CENTREDNESS AND ALTRUISM

(a) *Self-centredness*

It cannot be denied that self-love is admissible and legitimate, provided that it is in the right context. Indeed, a legitimate self-love is implicit in the Lord's commandment, 'Love your neighbour as yourself.' So the desire to develop fully as a person is quite valid. That man should 'strive to exist' and to foster his gifts and talents is equally consonant with the Gospel.

The trouble begins when the Ego makes itself the centre of life and the criterion of all moral conduct. We have to beware of the hypertrophy of the 'I' which a philosopher denounced as 'the myth of self-expansion'. The feeling of complacency, self-satisfaction and well-being that a person may experience is not a sufficient indication that he has found his true and authentic well-being, especially if one bears in mind that the actualization and blossoming of the Ego do not automatically correspond to the totality of the person, that 'complete personalism' which must take account of all the dimensions of the human being: the religious dimension, duration, continuity, social integration.

(b) *Altruism*

Self-absorption, as suggested, advocated or experienced in some training schools, basically disregards authentic altruism. If I love my neighbour because it makes me feel good to love him, I remain unconsciously locked in my own egoism. Sartre's remark that 'when you caress another person, you are invariably caressing yourself' may be existentially true to some extent, but if we stop there, we are ignoring and inhibiting the true gift of self and its gratuitousness.

In fact, this self-seeking love makes the subject allergic to his neighbour. The ego becomes literally autonomous, in other words it sets itself up as its own law. Referring to Bergson's *élan vital*, a scholar once pointed out that 'pure impulse' as a principle of nature does not automatically correspond to 'a pure impulse' in the moral sense.

In his book *Autrement qu'être*, the French philosopher Lévinas summed up his thinking in this rule of life: 'For others, in spite of myself, from myself'—a condensed message which psychotherapy centres would do well to display prominently.

And this holds true not only on the interhuman plane, but

also in man's direct encounter with the Other (capital letter), that is to say, with God.

As long as I go out to meet God starting from the 'I want' of my being, I will never encounter him as the Other, in Himself, but only as the other in reference to myself. The road to the worship of God remains blocked if we do not transcend ourselves. Besides, our true encounter with God is not unrelated to the way we encounter our fellow men.

Our love of God and our love of neighbour are so intimately connected that they cannot be dissociated with impunity.

I once came upon these thought-provoking lines (I cannot remember the source) which state the matter perfectly:

> I looked for my soul, but my soul I could not see.
> I looked for my God, but my God eluded me.
> I looked for my brother and I found all three.

An invitation not to isolate what God has united.

To conclude this chapter, I would like to quote a page by Professor Rezsohazy of the University of Louvain. Taken from his article entitled *The Neo-Individualists* (published in *La Libre Belgique*), it describes how widespread this phenomenon of hypertrophic egotism has become in today's world. His reflections will serve as a background to my previous remarks:

> This resurgence of individualism can, no doubt, be understood as a protest against a society composed of anonymous masses and not of human beings each endowed with a personal dignity and identity. A protest, too, against the prevalence of strict rules which prescribe what must be done instead of letting people freely pave the paths of their own destiny.
>
> But this ardently claimed faculty of choosing entails a preliminary search and the discovery of a model of happiness

towards which men should direct their steps. Well, contemporary man's quest is neither religious, nor philosophical, nor inspired by any social doctrine.

What attracts him is neither eternal salvation, nor a golden age, nor a coveted wisdom, but psychic security and social success, the momentary impression of personal well-being. This narcissistic quest, described by Christopher Lasch,[2] is observable in various domains, ranging from literature and art to the feminist movement. It is becoming tragic because it is afraid of old age and death. Surely this is an expression of despair on the part of a civilization incapable of coping with its own future?

Although the progress of these neo-individualistic tendencies contains obvious seeds of decadence, it cannot be halted by any decree. In my view, the reversal will take place when the absolute priority accorded to the search for self will have clearly demonstrated its harmful effects on society: the increasing debility of the family, the weakening of natural ties of fellowship, the multiplication of signs of escape from life's trials and responsibilities.

The crux of the problem lies in controlling the tension between each individual's aspiration to personal happiness and the need of our brothers and sisters to be loved as we love ourselves. To achieve this synthesis is to make a success of one's life. In historical terms, when a civilization finds the right balance between individual rights and social duties, it has reached its highest peak.

1. Homewood, Illinois, The Dorsey Press, 1982.
2. *The Culture of Narcissism* (New York, Norton, 1978).

IV

Is My Lived Experience the Supreme Criterion?

1. SUBJECTIVISM

What is of vital importance, we are told, when one begins these self-analyses is lived experience. Each subject is asked to concentrate on his actual lived experience and to explore it methodically and thoroughly. This dive into the ocean must be repeated again and again. The subject advances in this self-discovery by being actively docile to the successive sensations which enable the I–ego to progress. The analysis is completed when sensation has yielded all its content. The major assertion is that lived experience takes precedence over everything else.

So here we are, immersed in a subjectivism closed in on itself. My emotional feelings triumph and take over from my choices, my decisions, my successive commitments.

It is all very well to say that one feels this or that in one's heart, but if the heart is not educated, it can feel absolutely anything. So it is essential that a deeply rooted Christian understanding and wisdom should accompany and deepen the spontaneity and freedom of my feelings.

It is important not to confuse this listening to the self with the voice of the Spirit who speaks in the heart of our feelings. Interiority is an important dimension of all spiritual experience, but it must not be confused with a certain 'intimism' which might foster many illusions.

What is serious is that these fluctuations of the ego leave no room for a faithful commitment, whether in the consecrated religious life or in marriage. For why should I take on a lifelong commitment if tomorrow, or in ten years' time, my 'I' will have changed? 'We will never again have our soul of this evening', wrote the poetess Anna de Noailles despairingly.

2. TEMPORARY FAITHFULNESS

Faithfulness to previous commitments, whether conjugal or religious, seems to have very little weight when the course one adopts requires actual sensations to be the determining factor and the 'I' to be the supreme arbitrator.

With such a conception of freedom and time we are on shaky ground. For, in this optimistic light, the role of sin is minimized or wholly disregarded; Christian freedom is limited to letting what lies in the depth of my being rise to the surface. Morality is reduced to consenting to what my own being decrees. The criterion of moral rectitude is the feeling that I am following the dictates of my ego. It is fairly obvious that here we are overstepping the timely rehabilitation of the personal conscience—as urged by Vatican II—and indulging in a moral subjectivism which is all the more dangerous because it is founded above all on individual feelings.

We must also beware of the conception of *time* implicit in this pedagogy, for it is a thoroughly unreliable conception. Following the mainstream of today's culture (a mainstream typical of periods of crisis), many of our contemporaries are attempting to focus exclusively on the present moment: today is the only interesting and fruitful reality. For them it is a matter of 'living from day to day'; and for the Christian, it is a matter of being docile to a Spirit capable of only a fleeting, momentary action.

In so far as the experience of duration is one that most keenly tests human responsibility, it is understandable that attempts are made to neutralize it. But a Christian must never forget that Christianity is an historical religion, with its lasting glories and a final goal, and that it is therefore incompatible with a 'pointillist' conception of time.

Moreover, such a reaction to time is dangerous and demobilizing. A blind trust in the radiant influence of 'liberated' persons and groups might easily lead to a premature depreciation and devaluation of any pastoral or apostolic project whose success depends on continuity. This equally applies to many other spheres of activity.

3. THE PRIMACY OF EXPERIENCE

Is it true that experience is the supreme authority? And that my own experience is the criterion for judging the validity of all things? And that no idea, whether my own or another's, has as much weight as my experience? Is it true that, consequently, I must always refer to my experience in order to come closer and closer to the truth gradually developing in me? These are so many preliminary questions which have to be examined critically.

People readily assert that self-analysis belongs exclusively to the sphere of psychology and must take account of no other laws; which means in effect that reality must be its only starting point. 'Reality is my guru', they say. But this is clearly an unrealistic statement, for we would also need to know through what kind of spectacles the subject is looking at reality. And should he confine that reality to his personal experience, disregarding all the other aspects of the same reality, such as the communal or the institutional, which are also an integral part of reality?

Once this false postulate is adopted, a man will proclaim that his personal experience is the supreme criterion. But it is clear that if his experience is self-justifying, as he would have us believe, he must begin by throwing out any critical analysis contributed by others. Before he can accept it as a valid criticism, he must not only work through a course of self-analysis, privately or in a group, but also participate in a long series of experimental sessions, possibly as many as twenty, spread over several years.

This exorbitant requirement not only disqualifies any criticism from the outset, but also discounts any rational type of critical assessment. For it involves an implicit negation of the role of reason as man's guide. And according to the ancient and still valid definition of Aristotle, man is 'a reasoning animal', even if he is well aware that reality is not approached through reason alone. So although there can be no question of advocating a reductive rationalism, the fact remains that reason cannot be thrown out under the pretext that experience is the only valid guide.

Not only is it a mistake to waive reason aside, but true realism requires us to recognize that there must be a philosophy underlying these analyses and teachings that claim to be purely psychological, for no psychological fact can be isolated as a 'psychologically pure substance'.

To claim that human behaviour can be studied without reference to a philosophy, a theology or an ideology, is to relapse into the pragmatism whose chief exponent was William James, and which incorrectly applied verification, the law of the positive sciences, to domains which by definition eluded it.

I cannot understand *myself* without situating *myself* as a 'being-in-the-world', and without some metaphysical insight, be it conscious or unconscious.

Psychology becomes psychologism when it is accepted as a full and total explanation of what man experiences, or when it attaches excessive importance to the specifically psychological explanation. That this type of error is prevalent can be judged by the enthusiasm of those who fall prey to it. But, to quote Professor A. Vergote of the University of Louvain,

> The object of religious psychology is religion in so far as it affects the personality and society. This specificity of psychological comprehension is obtained at a price: it is never total. Psychology remains open in at least two directions: towards the psychological and towards the metaphysical. Often it has yielded to the temptation to refer back to itself in its attempt to provide explanations. The heuristic principle urges it to be total, to leave no blanks . . . Carried along by its desire for an ultimate foundation, it easily goes beyond its own boundaries and, contrary to its proper vocation, it tends to transform itself into either metaphysics or physiology.[1]

The assiduous participants in these analyses would do well to make a 'depth analysis' of the very limitations of their process and of what their 'feelings' are on the subject.

1. A. Vergote, *La psychologie religieuse* (Brussels, Dessart, 1966), pp. 15–16.

V

The True Self from the Christian Viewpoint

1. THE CHRISTIAN VIEWPOINT

Before speaking of the true self, let me explain what I mean by 'the Christian viewpoint'.

In order to discover his true self, the Christian must look at himself through the eyes of an Other: the eyes of Christ, who lives in him.

The drama of the Church today is that too few Christians still remember what their Christian 'being' really is. 'Christians, recognize your own dignity', said Pope Leo the Great to his people. His words still remain a pressing invitation. The rechristianization of Christians is an urgent priority at the moment.

Vatican Council II was a pastoral Council, concerned to adapt the Church to the pastoral needs of our time. Its working hypothesis was that the members of the Church were authentic Christians, or at least endeavoured to be. Well, twenty years later, the facts are obliging us to re-examine this premise. When we speak of Christians today, what kind of people, what kind of qualities, have we in mind?

This is a painful question. Is it true that, by and large, today's Christians believe with a personal, committed, convinced faith?

Inherited Christianity, which formerly rested on birth and education, must now increasingly become a faith founded on a personal decision, taken very consciously in adulthood.

Generally speaking, Christians are not blamed for being Christian, but for being insufficiently Christian. A merely practising Church does not suffice; it must be a confessing Church. We have to proclaim Jesus Christ in today's world and witness to our faith in Him. 'Everyone who acknowledges me before men,' said the Lord, 'I will also acknowledge before my Father.'

We need Christians who believe in Jesus, the only Son of the Father, who proclaim their faith in the Resurrection and in the mighty work of the Holy Spirit, and who embody their faith in every aspect of their lives.

We need Christians who know how to discover in their faith their true human identity, in the light of Jesus Christ. With rare insight, Pascal wrote: 'Not only do we know God through Jesus Christ alone, but we do not even know ourselves except through Jesus Christ. Apart from Jesus Christ we know not what is our life, or our death, or God, or what we ourselves are.'[1]

That is what I call the Christian viewpoint.

2. MAN IN THE LIKENESS OF GOD

For the Christian educator, every pedagogy aiming at man's growth is therefore conditioned by the image he carries within him of man, as God wishes man to be.

So it is important for him to understand, first of all, the real nature of man, as a being fashioned by the hands of his Creator, existing in the concrete reality of history after breaking the first Covenant, yet called to live out his own supernatural vocation. Before reaching into himself, man must lift up his eyes to God and question Him.

Here I am reminded of Chesterton's review of a book, entitled *What I Think about God*, by an author whose name I forget—let us call him Mr Jackson. With his inimitable wit, Chesterton reacted more or less along these lines: 'I have no doubt that it would be interesting to learn what Mr Jackson thinks of God, but it would be far more exciting, I'm sure, to discover what God thinks of Mr Jackson.'

This, indeed, is what the Christian's preference and initial approach should be. And it stands in sharp contrast with the lines written not so long ago by a Belgian educationist, Arnauld Clausse: 'Man is made in no one's likeness. It is up to him to create himself constantly . . . So the mind should no longer be regarded as the faculty of understanding and contemplation, but as an instrument for action . . . Its task is to create new truths by its own efforts.'[2]

In marked contrast to this total relativism, which is closed to any transcendental dimension and springs from the very negation of God, I would like to quote a few lines from a remarkable article by Father S. Decloux, S. J., Assistant General of the Jesuits. His article looks at the repercussions on the religious life of the theories propagated by those whom Paul Ricoeur calls the 'teachers of suspicion' (Marx, Nietzsche, Freud), and who all derived their inspiration from Feuerbach:

> The real issue in this debate is to understand what the true nature of man is; it requires us to ask ourselves if we ought not to reverse Feuerbach's assertion and say that the true mystery of anthropology is theology. We have not yet discovered man, and we do not know what we are saying when we speak of man, nor what we hope for man, if we have failed to grasp that, in the end, the true dimension of man's heart is God. What man can possess is nothing, if not God. What man can love is nothing, if not God. What he can want is nothing, if not God.
>
> So, in the final analysis, the debate is between anthropologies. Our task is to create a Christian anthropology in

which man can discover what his true dimension, his real depth, is: not simply the absolute depth of which Nietzsche spoke, but something other than the absolute of which I make myself the measure, and which must be wholly reassessed since it is mortal.

But if that absolute is the Absolute of God, we are instantly swept, within our hope, into the paschal mystery of Christ. What we live through in our history is quite simply the experience of being swept with him into that mystery. The reality of what we are, which must appear before God, and which is already revealed to us in God's light and by his Word, is the reality which the Son has enabled us to know by speaking to us of the Father and giving us his Spirit.[3]

3. WOUNDED, SINFUL MAN

Who am I? The answer is not simple, for there are various aspects within me which I have to take up simultaneously and which the Christian faith helps me to identify.

I am a being endowed with many gifts, but I am also a fragile, vulnerable creature, wounded by sin. In order to stand on my feet and to remain upright, I must begin by kneeling before God. We are a mixture of greatness and wretchedness. We accept neither the naturalistic optimism which disregards sin, nor fundamental, radical pessimism. Neither Jean-Jacques Rousseau, who asserts that man is naturally good, but disfigured by society, and that he must be left to his own resources in order to develop freely along the right lines; nor Luther and the pessimism of those who, in his wake, consider man to be fundamentally tainted by sin and justified solely by faith in God's saving grace. Neither Charybdis nor Scylla: here too we have to steer a safe course between two perils.

The very word 'sin' is understandable only in the light of

faith. 'According to its strict definition,' wrote Cardinal de Lubac, 'sin is a biblical and Christian concept; it implies not only the authority of a few transcendental laws, but a personal relationship between man and a personal God . . . Sin is not merely the rejection of a law—or even of a divine law—but also the rejection of God's summons to share his life.'[4]

Only faith can open our hearts and minds to the true dimension of sin. To suppress the awareness of sin under the pretext of being optimistic about man, because he is naturally good, is to erode a dimension of Christianity which lives by the covenant between God and man. It is also to ignore the whole mystery of the Cross: in the light of Jesus' death on Calvary, we discover what sin is in the eyes of God. By this I mean that the deicidal character of sin becomes apparent. The true responsibility for that death, which was nonetheless to triumph over all death, should not be laid upon the Jews or the Romans of Jesus' time: it must be sought in the sin of sinful humanity. Only in this light can we understand what sin is.

Here I could quote a number of pages from the book *Man a Sinner before God*, the work of an exegete, Mgr Bussini, Auxiliary Bishop of Grenoble. I have chosen a few significant extracts from it:

> We acquire a sense of sin only when we receive the revelation of God's faithfulness to us.
>
> Sin, in the strict sense, is present only when man freely closes himself to his Creator's prevenient Love.
>
> Each sinner is a member of sinful humanity. Through his personal sin, he collaborates in the collective work which is the sin of the world. Furthermore, he stands and falls with that sinful humanity even before he takes on a personal commitment. By that very fact, he is from birth in a state of estrangement from God, and a state of inner servitude from

which he would be unable to emerge had not Jesus given mankind free access to his Father.

Because of that solidarity between all men, humanity cannot be reduced to a sum of aligned individuals. It constitutes a 'we', with its own consistency and originality. Freedom and responsibility are not cancelled on that account. Quite the contrary. Because of the ties which unite me from birth with all men, I am called to ratify or to disapprove of what happens between them.

What constitutes the essence of original sin in us is the innate inability of man, unaided by Christ, to direct his existence through a fundamental choice consonant with God's will. This inability is, as it were, the seed of personal sins.

So I am speaking here of a wound in our freedom, which weakens it without doing away with it. By his death, Jesus ran counter to man's original disobedience and reversed the disastrous situation in which humanity found itself.[5]

We recognize that, without Christ, we would be in a state of alienation and servitude from which we could not free ourselves by our own efforts. We believe that the Spirit is 'the power of God saving all who have faith' (Rom. 1:16).

All this is an integral part of our Christian faith and it is incompatible with the Pelagian naturalism which we breathe in today, for it is in the very atmosphere of our time, and which is a negation of Christianity and of the mystery of the redeeming Cross.

Today, people no longer dare to say that there is a world for which Jesus did not pray, a world at variance with the Gospel. They no longer dare to speak of sin: sin is reduced to an 'error', a 'failing'. Tolstoy, in one of his novels, deliberately translated the expression 'remission of sins' by 'deliverance from errors'. I have myself heard the leader of a retreat reciting the rosary and conveying much the same idea by saying 'Pray for us, your children' instead of 'Pray for us sinners'. This evasiveness in regard to sin and the 'confiteor' does, in fact, suppress the very idea of redemption and salvation in the conscious mind.

The true source of Christian optimism is not the conviction that man is good provided that he is not perverted by society, but faith in the God who regenerates man and brings about in him a conversion which transforms his heart and opens it to the full breadth of God's Love at work in the person who welcomes it.

We cannot understand the eucharistic liturgy or our sacramental rites if we leave out the 'redemptive' and 'healing' aspects immanent in them. An 'innocent', 'euphoric' religion is neither realistic nor Christian. Christianity is a paschal religion precisely because it has lived through Good Friday in the person of its Head.

Only the saints have some understanding of the reality of sin, in the light of the Cross. They know what sin is because they have a deeper insight into God's Holiness, which Jesus himself gave us as a model of perfection (Mat. 5:48).

In my book *A New Pentecost*? (1975), I wrote these lines which, alas, are just as topical today:

> In the world in which we live, the phrase 'Jesus, Saviour' has become a problem. To know that I am saved, I must know that I have been saved from something. But from what? Faith tells us that Jesus came to save his people from the Law. St Paul proclaims over and over again liberation from a stifling legalism which holds man captive in a net of formal prescriptions and rituals; in the face of such slavery he asserts the true freedom of the children of God.
>
> Faith also teaches that Jesus came to save me from myself, from sin and death and the forces of evil. All of this has no meaning for someone who claims that man is self-sufficient,

> that sin does not exist, that there is nothing after death, and who dismisses the power of the evil one as an outdated myth. Jesus, whose name means 'Saviour', . . . cannot be recognized as such unless we know what it is from which we have been saved. Recently a speaker on television, who professed to be a Christian, declared: 'I refuse to be "saved", 'I want to be "liberated".' He forgot that salvation and liberation are closely linked: in saving man from sin, the root of all evil, both individual and collective, Jesus established the basis of all forms of liberation of which we are in need. To free the oppressed, to struggle against violence and injustice, are among the blessings of salvation, as the entire Old Testament had already proclaimed.[6]

Any Christian pedagogy of human growth which disregards or leaves out these three interrelated aspects of man, which must be respected as a unity, can only be a distorted and dangerously euphoric teaching with no roots in reality.

4. MAN SAVED AND LIBERATED

In Christian circles there has been much discussion about the duty of incarnating the love of God, as a consequence of the very mystery of the Incarnation of God's Son. But there have been few attempts to stress that the Incarnation itself was a Redemptive Incarnation. Jesus came into the world to be fully one of us, a man among men, and at the same time to save man from himself.

In his first public address after his election, Pope John Paul II made this unforgettable appeal to the crowd in St Peter's Square: 'Do not be afraid to welcome Jesus Christ: he is man's Redeemer.'

The eclipse of the sense of sin has led Christians to blur this redeeming aspect of Christ's mission.

We have to rediscover the meaning of the expression 'to receive grace'. For the word 'grace' has a double meaning: it signifies both the grace that elevates nature to the supernatural and 'the receiving of a free pardon'. The latter meaning sheds light on a new dimension of grace: that of sin forgiven.

So the word grace refers not only to the free gift of God that elevates and transforms nature, but also to a change of heart, a change in our innermost being, restored by God.

To be 'transfigured', sinful nature has to 'turn back' to God.

In fact, the Gospel opens with this call which resounds through the Bible. It is also the call that rings through Peter's first missionary address in Jerusalem: 'You must repent' (Acts 2:38).

In this new and truly Christian perspective, we must say plainly that, if the union of nature and the supernatural is achieved, in principle, in the mystery of the Incarnation, the union of nature and grace can be fulfilled only in the mystery of the Redemption.

5. MAN LOVED BY GOD

By definition, a Christian is someone who believes in God's love. 'We ourselves have known and put our faith in God's love for us,' said St John (1 John 4:16). The Christian believes that God loves him in a personal, unique and perfect way.

The whole of Scripture proclaims God's perseverance and faithfulness in Love. Now as in the past, God lives this fidelity not only as an intense commitment to mankind's 'today', but also with the passionate continuity of a liberating Love.

Far too many Christians dare not believe in this personal love of God, this first, constant love that never weakens and envelops every human existence. Often the reason for their incredulity is the fact that they have never encountered, in their family or on their path, believers whom they could see as a reflection of the divine fidelity.

Recently a youth chaplain said that he was very struck by the fact that many young people today find it difficult to believe that God loves them personally. They are beset by anxieties, worried over the future, insecure.

To know that one is loved by God—Father, Son and Holy Spirit—with this triple and unique love, is an overwhelming discovery that opens up new horizons and orients one's whole life.

Faith reveals to us, moreover, that God not only loves us, as we are, but wants to act within us as that 'power of loving' which makes us love our fellow men—and we are called to love them *with* the love of God, *with* God's own heart.

'When you love,' wrote the poet Kahlil Gibran, 'you should not say "God is in my heart", but rather "I am in the heart of God" ' (*The Prophet*).

This is indeed my own vital conviction: it resides in him, not in me. It protects me from all my vacillations.

1. Blaise Pascal, *Pensées* (London, Dent, 1960), p. 172.
2. *Une doctrine socialiste de l'éducation*, pp. 122–4.
3. From the review *Vie Consacrée*, no. 4, 1978, pp. 224–5.
4. H. de Lubac, *Petite catéchèse sur nature et grâce* (Paris, Communion Fayard, 1980), pp. 92 and 120.
5. *L'homme pécheur devant Dieu* (Paris, Cerf, 1978), pp. 36, 49, 85, 99, 114.
6. *A New Pentecost?* (New York, Seabury Press, 1975), pp. 115–16.

VI

Underlying Doctrinal Problems concerning God

Glancing through humanistic expositions addressed to a Christian public, I have come upon quite a few underlying problems relating to God, the Trinity and the Church and advancing ambiguous propositions. Here I would like to analyse a few of these statements which are particularly important from the doctrinal viewpoint.

To begin with, let us acknowledge that there is nothing wrong with a natural human relation which takes man as its starting-point and endeavours to find God. Freud's fundamental error was that he envisaged God as a mere illusion, an internalized image of the human father—a loving or vindictive father, depending on one's personal experience, but leading to a 'collective neurosis': religion. During the 50s, Viktor Frankl contradicted the master and rectified this view by demonstrating the universal existence of a spiritual unconscious, animated by a desire for meaningfulness which strains towards God. He stated that every man is naturally a religious being (*homo religiosus*).

Philosophers (e.g. Leibniz) have also taken man as their starting-point and endeavoured to reach God by the method of *theodicy*, which is a search for God assisted by reason alone, but falls short of theology, since the latter conducts its search in the light of faith. The God whom men seek in a groping fashion with the aid of reason alone cannot hide the face of the true God, who far transcends our approximations and must be sought endlessly.

When we are addressing Christians, the progress from theodicy to the theology of Revelation calls for a precise and strictly accurate vocabulary. It is not easy to make a rocket sent from the ground (reason) link up with another sent from Above (faith), but the rendezvous is too important to be missed.

1. GOD—WHAT ABSOLUTE HAVE WE IN MIND?

First of all, we must ask ourselves what exactly the humanist means when he speaks of man's relation to the Absolute. To what 'inner Absolute' is he referring?

The natural experience of God 'discovered in one's innermost being' can give rise to quite a few ambiguities. Why?

—Seeing clearly into myself is not a sufficient reason for claiming that I have found God there.

—'Being at peace with myself' does not mean that I have already found God. We know that, psychologically speaking, quite a few saints were not in the least at peace with themselves!

—Being docile to the forces of life welling up in me is not necessarily an indication that I have found God. St Paul, and Holy Scripture with him, prefer to follow another 'natural' path to God: it resides in the contemplation of his wonders in the world around us and in the many splendours of his creation.

—In any case, God lies beyond the depths of my being, beyond any name we give him, beyond the place we assign to him.

When we claim to have discovered in our innermost being the reality of the inner Absolute, who sweeps us out of ourselves towards something greater, towards a fullness of being and life which lies beyond us, yet is homogeneous with our selves and enables us to apprehend the infinity of our being, how should we understand that reality which is said to be both immanent and transcendent? Are we still speaking of a God 'distinct' from his creature, wholly immanent, of course, but thanks to an authentic transcendence?

The Christian vision of God cannot be confined within these limits; it rejects the idea of homogeneity with the human being and his limitations. The inspired writings proclaim that the transcendence of the God of revelation is of a wholly other nature.

Although I experience the reality of my being, it does not follow that, simultaneously with this experience, I can enter into an intuitive knowledge of God. Liberating my being does not mean liberating 'God' in me. All these formulas are, to say the least, ambiguous and must be clarified.

The God whom man awaits and seeks as the fulfilment of his desire for complete personal growth cannot be identified with the God of faith and Revelation who bursts into our history, summons us and disconcerts us.

When we overemphasize God's immanent aspect, we must never lose sight of his transcendence: these two aspects are simultaneous and complete each other.

It is said that the believer must 'live God' as a direct, personal experience: this expression conspicuously narrows down the otherness of God and seriously underestimates the difference between God and man. Here it seems that the Creator's function is reduced to that of a 'stop-gap': he is there to gratify the deep needs of his creature.

Admittedly, once man acknowledges God's otherness, he has the painful task of reassessing himself and of discovering his sinfulness—an uncomfortable experience which, according to some, even the Christian should be spared.

Lastly, let us note that the concept of Absolute is singularly broad and hazy if it designates everything that comes from within man and urges him towards a 'more' (but not towards an Other!). In my view, it is hazardous to place God, even as a temporary measure, in the same category of Absolute as Love, Justice, Liberty and so on. This way of thinking creates ambiguities, and it has nothing to do with an authentic apologetic of his otherness. It involves sacrificing the originality of the God of Jesus Christ, who cannot be reduced to those other 'absolutes'. God's Face cannot be trivialized.

The God of our faith is not an undemanding father who simply appeals to us and draws us to him. In him Truth and Love are inseparably united.

Even when the mystique of 'myself and Being' is restored to the purely philosophical plane, it is not elucidated and buttressed by a precise metaphysic of the causality of the created being and of his participation in the Increate. When it refers to God (the Father) as the founding origin of the created being, the latter does not appear to be finalized by God, understood as both the efficient and the final cause, the Creator of the human being's very source and goal.

Such a natural pseudo-mystique of being is, in the final analysis, a perverted mystique. Its way of enabling the human being's mission to unfold is to send man back constantly to his natural condition and to keep him there. Thus the flowering of his innermost being (perceived in terms of sentiments and emotions) becomes the theoretical and practical measure of the human vocation. The supernatural is reinterpreted accordingly and reduced to the affective life of the self.

In these circumstances 'the mission of being' in which the created self finds fulfilment does not lead on to the expectation of 'the things that no eye has seen, nor ear heard, all that God has prepared for those who love him' (1 Cor. 2:9).

2. CHRIST, THE SAVIOUR OF MAN

Here we should reread John Paul II's magnificent appeals to humanity not to fear Jesus Christ but to accept him as the true Saviour, man's salvation, since he alone knows man's innermost being.

To assert that man is saved by man is to make an ambiguous, false statement that leaves out the dimension of 'grace'.

There is no evidence of Christian thinking in the assertion that the mission of pedagogy and psychology is to show men and society the path of salvation and that they can find their way to salvation with the help of other men who have already been saved and have become the saviours of their brothers. The very least that can be said of this view is that it is a misuse of language.

The Christian interpretation of salvation is that it is primarily the sanctification achieved in man through the gift of divine grace. It is that gift which saves us. Of course, grace calls for a kind of 'translation' of our spiritual values in every sphere of life, including the psychological. And with nuances and careful qualifications, such a translation can be called 'salvation', but in a secondary and analogical sense. The same is true of socio-political liberation.

A perverted naturalistic mystique which disregards the deep meaning of the word 'salvation' also ignores, by the same token, the mediation of Christ the Saviour.

It is not enough to speak of Christ as an example: in Christ our faith recognizes the one through whom, with whom and in whom we receive the Holy Spirit and gain access to the Father.

His sacrificial and priestly mediation cannot be passed over in silence. For here the whole paschal mystery is at stake.

The Cross and Christ's obedience unto death on the Cross are, as it were, the 'indispensable' passage from this world to God. And once silence is maintained on the subject, the whole sacramental mystery of the Church, as the ongoing mediation of Jesus Christ, becomes blurred and risks being forgotten—not necessarily by the present generation, but by tomorrow's youth, who will no longer live on the great achievements of the past.

The Creator's presence can, of course, be found by resorting to being. For Christians, however, the chosen path of encounter with the Father is not 'that interiority' and no more. It is not the path of being, but their life-giving communion with divine grace.

Jesus Christ is the Way. Therefore the way cannot be the created being alone. Christians cannot accept this 'reduction' of God's life to the life of the human being as such.

To reduce the mission of Jesus Christ and, in his wake, of the Church to that of serving humanity by giving it some extra assistance in the 'formation of the human being', or to that of helping people to know themselves, to realize their personality and to act as their feelings dictate, is to be poles apart from Christianity; it is an invitation to follow a new path of salvation.

To assert that the true religion is the one that best reveals man to himself and enables him to find the highest self-fulfilment by being faithful to the best in himself is to see the human being only as a human being and to ignore his Christian dimension.

What becomes, in the circumstances, of all the positive data we have welcomed as followers of Christ?

What happens to the reality of grace, original sin, the redemption, Jesus Christ, the Church, the sacraments, the certainty of eternal life?

And this list could be extended much further. For if we

envisage the whole work of salvation in this context of affective naturalism, is it anything more than a 'Christian reading' of Carl Roger's analysis?

Surely a Christian must know that communion with God, through grace, transfigures him and enables him to share in the divine life. It affects his whole personality. That 'self-fulfilled' man is promised the joy of heaven.

3. THE PELAGIAN CONTROVERSY

Pelagius (*c.* 360–430 AD), an Irish lay monk, who crossed from Rome to North Africa, has left deep imprints on our time. The Pelagian controversy was the first great controversy of Western Christendom. In a sense, it has dominated the whole of Western theology. It has been said that the discussions surrounding Protestantism and Jansenism were, in the main, but a reiteration of those that took place in North Africa at the beginning of the fifth century. It was within and through this controversy that the West addressed the question of Christianity's very significance and the meaning of the Redemption.

For, in the naturalism of Pelagius, Christ practically loses his place as the Saviour. According to Pelagius, man is naturally good: it is up to him to complete the divine work of creation. Man, he asserts, must be aware of his natural ability to keep the divine commandments. Nature is of prime importance, and in relation to nature Christ plays but a secondary role. Man saves himself by living in accordance with nature. It follows that Christianity is but a natural religion, though better and more perfect than the other world religions. Pelagius says explicitly that Christ came to make man a better human being.[1]

This whole theory challenges the Church's doctrine on original sin, infant baptism and the very meaning of man's Redemption.

When asked if it was possible for man to live without sin and to keep all the commandments of God, Pelagius replied: 'Not only can he achieve this ideal . . . but it is his duty to do so.'

Conversely, the anti-Pelagian theory of St Augustine proclaims both the absolute 'metaphysical' possibility of keeping the divine commandments and the 'historical' impossibility of so doing without grace. Finding the right balance between two extremes is always a delicate problem: some will yield to the optimism of Pelagius and dismiss the whole of St Paul's teaching on the universality of sin (Rom. 1:3), while others will fall prey to a radical pessimism and assert that human nature is wholly corrupt and irresistibly drawn to sin. Throughout the centuries the Church has helped us to maintain the right balance between the role of nature and the role of grace; but when Christians place too much emphasis on one to the detriment of the other, the Church is obliged to redress the balance and to stress their complementarity.

At the present moment the wind is blowing so fiercely in the Pelagian direction that we are duty-bound to underline the role of God's redemptive grace.

1. *Letter to Demitriades*, C. III, P. 4 xxx, 18.

VII

Underlying Doctrinal Problems concerning Man

1. WHAT DO WE MEAN BY 'HUMAN NATURE'?

The humanistic school replies that human nature is man's fundamental nature, and that when it is allowed to function freely, it is constructive, valid and trustworthy. The humanist takes the confident view that man can trust his reactions: they will be positive and dynamic by the mere fact that by relying on them, man becomes profoundly himself.

Despite a few variations found in the teachings of his disciples, Carl Rogers, the great exponent of this theory, maintains that man has a manifest, or at least latent, ability to understand himself and to solve his problems well enough to ensure his own growth and to function effectively as a human being.

Carl Rogers' followers, too, are distinguished by their constant determination to tone down the dimension of egoism and aggression which is present in both the individual and the group of which he forms part.

The permanent displaying of the 'wealth' of each individual, the encouragement to marvel at oneself and others—all such practices are in direct contradiction not only with our everyday experience as human beings, but also with the most reliable contemporary anthropology.

All this is a far cry from Christ's Gospel, which does not teach that kind of absolute self-confidence and optimism. Scripture proclaims that the Powers of Evil are at work in the human race, that every man is a sinner and needs redemption. It shows the greatness of man, but also his weakness, his original wound, which leaves its mark on the whole person and, in a sense, affects all his actions. Whereas Protestants would call it 'corruption', Catholics would say 'wound'; but no Catholic can advocate the complete optimism that is basic to this new gospel—a gospel alien to the Church's tradition.

Rogers, incidentally, was very conscious of the revolutionary and anti-Christian character of his 'discoveries'. And he wrote these lines:

> One of the most revolutionary concepts to grow out of our clinical experience is the growing recognition that the innermost core of man's nature, the deepest layers of his personality, the base of his 'animal nature', is positive in nature—is basically socialized, forward-moving, rational and realistic.
>
> This point of view is so foreign to our present culture that I do not expect it to be accepted, and it is indeed so revolutionary in its implications that it should not be accepted without thorough-going inquiry. But even if it should stand these tests, it will be difficult to accept.[1]

2. WHAT DOES 'BEING WHOLLY MYSELF' MEAN?

The fullness of life to which every man aspires resides, we are told, in being wholly oneself: tender, considerate of others, cooperative, but also on occasion lazy, sensual and hostile. The free expression of these tendencies results in a total harmony of man's being: the process is bound to be positive, constructive, realistic and totally reliable. To live, say these humanists, is to progress. The individual's growth is achieved in a naturally harmonious way. Since life is a positive force, it is, by its very nature, more contagious than evil. Any attempt to fence it in or to cast it in a rigid mould is harmful.

Underlying this 'reading' of the human being is a certain vitalism, possibly influenced by nineteenth-century evolutionism and its view that everything is animated by a life force, an ascending movement relentlessly producing a fullness, a harmonious fulfilment of being.

From this standpoint only one task is assigned to our freedom and to the education that fashions it: that of letting the vital forces constantly expand without interference. Such a teaching encourages a mainly passive and quietist view of the upbuilding of humanity, society and the Church. And, in the circumstances, there is a great danger that some authoritarian personalities might take advantage of that docility.

Furthermore, the 'new' is thought to be beneficial. It seems that stabilization does not exist in the humanistic universe; still less are regressions likely to occur there, except as harmless accidents. Evil and its attendant problems are, if not totally ignored, at least greatly relativized. Death, suffering and sin are practically absent from that world.

It is difficult to see how such a theory can help individuals and groups to build themselves up in any permanent sense and to cope effectively with the realities of everyday life.

This, at any rate, is not the philosophy that Christians find in the inspired writings. Scripture does not present the Christian life as an existence whose total harmony resides in being wholly oneself: cooperative and considerate of others, but also on occasion lazy, sensual and hostile.

We may ask ourselves whether even psychology advocates self-direction and the blossoming of the ego as the only supreme norm.

In his outline of genetic religious psychology, Professor A. Vergote writes of the adult:

> Two interrelated elements define the essence of adulthood: creative freedom and the acknowledgement of reality and others. This means that the adult is, in fact, he who manages to free himself, to some extent, of his psychological determinisms and to transcend his inner world, made up of drives and emotional demands. The adult has, so to speak, broken through the wall of psychologism. Adult religion consummates the rupture between God and man's psychic drives. It has transvaluated psychological religiosity.[2]

3. WHAT KIND OF AUTONOMY?

Disregarding all the conditionings that once influenced or still affect individual lives, the humanistic school asks each person to try to conduct his life autonomously, on his own responsibility . . . Every man must gradually come to trust his intuitions, and therefore himself. Thus all will discover that 'doing what their feeling tells them is right' will ultimately be a competent and reliable guide to really satisfactory conduct. How then can they agree with those who rely on directive principles, on a code of conduct drawn up by a group or an institution, on the judgement of others?

Do these assertions—which, incidentally, are very normative in their own fashion—comply even with the requirements of psychoanalysis?

For the Christian, Christ instituted a way of life with its own principles of direction and conduct, and these are summed up in the Gospel's ethical teaching. The Christian community, too, has directive ministries serving the various forms of Christian ideal based on the Gospel. Autonomy—which is, in fact, required of an adult person—must remain 'open' to what comes from Christ through the Church, whereas here it is locked in its own 'intuitions', and therefore closed in on itself.

4. WHAT KIND OF FULLNESS OF LIFE?

The 'fullness of life' process, say its exponents, involves the exploration and development of the human being's full potential. It involves the courage to exist and to plunge into the stream of life. This full life is not static, frozen and rigid. The advocates of the process do not seem in any way disturbed by the fact that the human being changes from one day to the next, that his feelings also change, and that his behaviour is not always consistent . . . A real journey into the unknown!

The Christian faith has a different tone of voice. When the inspired writings speak of fullness of life, they refer to life in communion with God, the Word and the Spirit. This fullness of life is a divine gift which matures in every person made godlike by grace. It is an adventure in God, according to his eternal purpose: that of leading us to this definitive, glorious and eternal fullness of life of the chosen. There lies the true mystery of the Christian adventure.

1. C. Rogers, *On Becoming a Person* (London, Constable, 1967), pp. 90–1.
2. A. Vergote, *La psychologie religieuse* (Brussels, Dessart, 1966), pp. 319–20.

VIII

Growth of the Christian

1. CHRISTIAN MATURITY

For us, man's vocation means both man's Christian vocation and the Christian's human vocation. It is with this central vision as our starting-point that we have to analyse the Christian's growth and respect its imperatives.

(a) *The necessity of selflessness*

During a youth retreat, one of my friends, a Scottish bishop, summed up our duty to ourselves as follows: 'Know yourself, love yourself, forget yourself.' This triple imperative does, in fact, comply simultaneously with all the aspects to be respected.

Know yourself: long ago Socrates gave this advice to his disciples. Self-knowledge, properly understood, is a perfectly legitimate form of self-love. The Lord himself gave his disciples the commandment to love one another 'as themselves'. So there is a legitimate and necessary self-love which has to be respected and fostered.

But this self-love does not imply self-centredness. On the contrary, it requires us to make the best possible use of the gifts we have received and to bring our talents to fruition. There is a false humility which amounts to falsehood, but there is also a self-assertion which can take the form of truth, courage and service.

This duty to love ourselves implies the duty to cultivate ourselves, to develop our inner wealth. As Louis Lavelle pointed out: 'The greatest gift we can make others is not to communicate our riches to them, but to help them discover theirs.' Paradoxically, it is by giving oneself that one finds oneself and opens out to the growing possibilities of self-giving.

But the Lord also uttered other, apparently contradictory, words when he made the duty of forgetting oneself central to self-love: 'He who finds his life will lose it, and he who loses his life for my service will find it' (Matt. 10:39).

And St Paul was to echo the Lord's words when he urged the Christians of Rome to 'go into the tomb': 'When we were baptized in Christ Jesus, we were baptized in his death; we went into the tomb with him . . . so that we too might lead a new life' (Rom. 6:3).

These are powerful expressions: Christianity draws its strength from that radicalism which 'off-centres' the self, knocks the selfish ego off its perch, and leaves a void so that an Other-than-us can enter and fill us with his Life. This self-renunciation in no way contradicts that legitimate self-love, the development of one's potential, but it gives it another, infinitely vaster and higher finality. It is an opening on to the infinite which grows out of dying to oneself. This double requirement must be kept not only in mind, but also—and simultaneously—in the heart: the disappearance of the 'I', the fracturing of the monadic ego of which Leibniz spoke, and the welcoming of the Other, that is to say, of the Spirit of Jesus who wishes to 'spiritualize' us in depth.

In the end, this path helps us to understand St Paul's triumphant cry: 'I live—not I, but Christ in me!' This is the Christian paradox which we have to live. Selflessness is central to life and love, as also to the authentic blossoming of the real self. It has been said that 'a life is great when it is dominated by concern for others'. Let us bear this in mind when we are attempting to chart the course of all human, and *a fortiori* Christian, growth.

Here I am reminded of a real episode which I once read about. It seems that an American undergraduate had placed on his desk a stone with the inscription 'You Are Third'. Urged by his fellow-students to explain what these words meant, he ended up by admitting that the stone was a present from his mother, who had asked him never to part with it, so that he would always remember that God came first, other people came next, and he came third.

With this triple imperative as a reminder, we too can safely advance along the path of self-exploration, for then it will be free of rubble and clearly signposted.

(b) *Openness is essential*

To underline God's immanence in man and to elaborate a threshold apologetic starting from man's personal experience is, as I said earlier, a legitimate path to God.

This method can adduce St Augustine as its authority, and especially his famous words: 'You have made us for yourself, O Lord, and our heart is restless until it finds its rest in you.'

In me I find 'natural' aspirations to happiness, to an everlasting life and love extending beyond space and time. And it is quite acceptable for a pedagogy to start from that point in order to lead man to God, the final and complete answer to his aspirations. This pedagogy is consonant with a Christian anthropology.

As is well known, the whole of Blondel's philosophical work was animated by this search for God in man's heart and actions. And before him, at the pastoral level, Cardinal Deschamps, Archbishop of Malines at the time of Vatican Council I, had elaborated a similar method. (Blondel, incidentally, acknowledged his indebtedness to that forerunner.) Such an approach is of value in that, starting from man's aspirations, it can awaken his need for the infinite and the absolute, thus guiding him towards God. But an introduction cannot claim to be the end of the search, even temporarily.

It is a 'threshold' method in that it prepares the way for faith. Faith itself comes from elsewhere. Faith is born of a Word communicated by God and received by man. That Word summons each one of us. It is a call that demands an answer, an action of God who asks us to adhere to his Word. It is that Word which judges us and not my subjectivity: my lived experiences, my feelings, my preferences. God has opened his heart to us in his Word, and our Christian life consists in responding to that Love, that freely offered covenant.

(c) *The necessity of integrating nature with grace*

The Christian self is not composed of two superimposed layers: nature on the one hand, grace on the other.

Historically speaking, there is no purely natural order in which man has not been called to a 'superhuman' life and to communion with the Triune God.

The hypothesis of a purely natural order—an order of creation—may have been considered a feasible proposition, but it has never been confirmed in fact. From the very beginning of Creation, man has been constituted in the supernatural order, and it is in this perspective that we have to harmonize what belongs to human nature *per se* with what belongs to our supernatural elevation, our full vocation.

Speaking of man raised to the supernatural order, Karl Rahner writes: 'Man's elevation to the supernatural is the absolute—though gratuitous—fulfilment of a being that cannot be "defined", that is to say, "delimited" in the manner of nonhuman beings, because he is spirit and transcendence towards the Absolute Being.'

It is a matter of respecting the whole of man in the real human being. Here I am speaking of the new man in Jesus Christ, and of a supernatural life inherent in his human life, yet transcending it. The supernatural is that divine element which man cannot attain by his human efforts, but which unites with man, whom it elevates, by penetrating him in order to divinize him, thus becoming, as it were, an attribute of the 'new man'. And though man's supernatural life can never be reduced to nature, it is deeply rooted in his innermost being.

Between nature and grace there is a relationship of reciprocity in unity, and we must never disregard it in the concrete circumstances of our everyday life.

2. DANGERS TO BE AVOIDED

If we wish to experience in the fullest sense that necessary integration of natural with supernatural growth, certain requirements must be respected and certain dangers avoided.

(a) *First danger: neutralism*

Jacques Maritain has written a well-known book whose title, *Distinguish to Unite*, also expresses its aim. What holds true of philosophy equally applies to pedagogy: the educator has to distinguish various levels of growth, but constantly endeavour to unite them in the real person, whose being is an indivisible unity.

In order to determine the process I intend to follow, I must know from the very beginning who is that 'Self' whom I am about to analyse. If I am dealing with a baptized person, I cannot regard his Christian being as purely incidental. If I am guiding a Christian, I cannot use a 'general purpose' method, valid for believers and non-believers alike. Neutralism is quite out of place here and, by the same token, a 'neutral' non-denominational school is not usually suited to the education of Christian children.

For in pedagogy, too, one cannot disregard metaphysics and theology with impunity. Proudhon already pointed out in the last century that 'at the root of every political problem lies a theological problem'. This statement is equally applicable to psychology, which cannot be surreptitiously transformed into psychologism, and still less into a religion. Paul C. Vitz, Professor of Psychology in the University of New York, has written a penetrating book on the subject, entitled *Psychology as Religion: the Cult of Self-Worship*. One cannot but rejoice that such a perceptive critique has emanated from the professional milieu itself.

For the Christian, the human without Jesus Christ is not the human according to God. It is not enough to say: 'Let's leave out this dimension; we're conducting this analysis with our own tools.' From the Christian viewpoint, such an analysis would be distorted from the start, because it is mutilated and cut off from its vital point of reference: Jesus Christ who said to us: 'I am the Way, the Truth and the Life.'

This saying of Jesus also holds true for whoever wishes to discover the path leading to self-knowledge (in the light of God), to his deep truth (in the eyes of God, who alone knows and scrutinizes the depths of man), and to the true life, which does not reveal itself to the Christian as the fruit of his introspection, but gradually emerges out of his faithfulness to the Gospel's teaching on living and dying to himself. And we are inevitably betraying our own faithfulness if we allow ourselves to be guided merely by egocentric feelings and aspirations, with all their subjective, fluctuating and ephemeral implications.

(b) *Second danger: giving priority to humanism*

Atheistic humanism is obviously not compatible with the Christian faith, but there is an even more subtle form of humanism which Christians must analyse carefully in order not to succumb to it. I would call it a 'priority humanism', by which I mean that it is an option expressed in the following terms: let us humanize man *first of* all, and *then* proceed to evangelize or christianize him. The 'first of all' and 'then' are the crux of the problem. On which of the two needs should the emphasis be placed? Am I first of all a man ('man be human, this is your first duty', said Rousseau) and then a Christian? Or am I primarily a Christian through my baptism, and then led—because I am a Christian—to be fully human as the fruit of my Christianity?

What comes first in Christian logic, always bearing in mind that the two aspects are inseparably united?

This question crops up periodically and it has to be clarified. In bygone days it gave rise to the Montuclard controversy and the *Christian Youth* movement. From the same angle it is basic to the theology of liberation. We have to examine it carefully, not in order to sacrifice any of its inherent values, but to recognize the theological order of priority, which does not exclude a simultaneous development in practice, but illuminates it and gives it coherence in the light of faith.

To wish to 'humanize first, then evangelize' is to lapse into a type of humanistic naturalism which does not comply with all the requirements of Christianity.

Some years ago, I devoted a chapter of my book *The Gospel to Every Creature* to this very question, in order to point out the anti-Christianity which is latent in such an option on the pastoral and missionary plane.

What is true on the social level remains valid on the personal level: there is no room for that 'first be human, then be Christian'. In the final analysis, such an option disregards the very character of the incarnate Christ, true man and true God. It overlooks the fact that no one was more human than Jesus Christ, and that a complete humanism springs from him as a flower from its root. The duties of humanizing and christianizing must command our attention simultaneously—this is an important point. But it must be stressed that simultaneity is compatible with two different rates of progress, as I pointed out in *The Gospel to Every Creature*:

> It is important indeed to understand the two different rates of progress which mark religious activity, according as it is considered in itself or in its temporal effects, i.e. its incarnation.
>
> The neglect of this distinction would seem to be the cause of the conflicting trends. To the school which preaches 'social service first', it is not right to oppose the doctrine of 'religious apostolate first', as if the two duties were to be considered on the one plane, and classified in order of time. But we must emphasize definitely the immediate or rapid nature of the christianization of men, contrasted with the slow movement of humanization. This is due not to the will of men but to the nature of things. A child is baptized: immediately grace floods his soul; if he dies on the evening of his baptism, he is fixed for all eternity as a full-grown Christian: he has received in one outpouring the plenitude of Christ. Such is the action of grace, interpreting the impatient love of God. But to grow up, to learn, to become a man, that child will require many years, according to the normal play of human factors. A man receives Holy Communion: a single host received with faith is sufficient to produce the immediate sacramental effect. But on the human plane, a gradual assimilation of varied food is required for nourishment. A sinner is converted: his discovery of God or his conversion may have taken place in a flash. 'Lord, you have become someone

for me all of a sudden', cries Claudel. Repentance works a transformation from sin to grace in one impulse, but to repair the harm done or to struggle successfully against rooted habits may take a lifetime.

These examples show that, when Christ takes possession of a man, the supernatural influence will act instantaneously, but the effect of that influence on his whole being and on the sphere in which he moves will follow a slow progression, ever retarded by the combined play of natural factors, personal and social.

Our Lord himself compared the Kingdom of Heaven to a measure of leaven which is mixed with three measures of flour and causes the dough to rise. When we have fully appreciated the slow nature of this process, which is due, not to God, but to normal secondary causes, we need not fear to emphasize the necessary link between the evangelization and the humanization of the world. The unequal rate of progress of the two movements will no longer disconcert us and we shall better perceive their profound harmony.[1]

An understanding of these two different rates of growth, which must be respected simultaneously, will help the Christian in search of a good training method to avoid giving priority to humanism, and to comply with the demands made upon him by his baptism.

1. *The Gospel to Every Creature* (London, Burns and Oates, 1956), pp. 24–5.

IX

Methods of Growth, in Christian Analysis

No one would deny the usefulness of self-knowledge, since it helps man to realize his potential and his latent gifts. So we must acknowledge that some methods of approaching and investigating the self are valid. But the real problem lies in determining how far a given approach is dependent on, or influenced by, an underlying naturalistic philosophy.

Here we are reminded, by analogy, of the discussions surrounding the liberation theologies, which—in their vocabulary, at least—are sometimes barely distinguishable from a Marxist sociological analysis. An error is dangerous only because of the part of truth it contains: so we must be careful to spot the ambiguities. And we must not believe that by declaring that he is doing pure psychology, a man can dodge the theological or philosophical issues underlying his teaching.

It is always advisable to analyse every method, whatever its nature, from the angle of its ultimate goal, from the angle of its successful integration into the whole Christian way of life and, more particularly, from the angle of the sacramental practice that accompanies the Christian throughout his life.

1. THE METHOD, FROM THE ANGLE OF ITS ULTIMATE AIM

In order to achieve its full Christian stature and to discern its path of progress, every method of growth must take account of the aim it is pursuing and discern its ways and means in relation to its aim.

What is the Christian seeking to achieve? What is the ultimate goal to which he will direct his attempts at self-development? What is that humanity which he is endeavouring to foster in himself and in the world?

We cannot subscribe to a humanistic, utopian and unrealistic type of vision, which requires man to achieve a kind of superhumanity here below. When I read that this or that method aims to 'bring about the new heaven and new earth promised by God, and to which men aspire', I am obliged to reject this unrealistic utopian dream, in no way promised by the Lord. That dream would be a kind of temporal messianism. Were it to dominate our horizon, such an aim, born of fantasy, would put us on the wrong track: the goal of our Christian journey does not lie there. Let us not get hold of the wrong ideal. Neither Jean-Jacques Rousseau nor Pelagius is compatible with our faith.

As to the method itself, it would be equally naturalistic to present our work of personality development as a strategy depending solely on our efforts. We cannot create the impression, even as a temporary and methodological strategy, that it is we who achieve our own maturation, by our own strength, by the company we keep and the aids we resort to, or by our repeated self-analyses.

Christian realism also obliges us to take account, at every stage of our spiritual development, of the realities of Evil which impede our progress.

In plain words, we must acknowledge that we are sinners, in our daily poverty, and humbly ask God, as we make our way, to preserve us from all evil, including the Powers of Evil.

Here I would like to repeat what I attempted to make clear in *Renewal and the Powers of Darkness*. We are afraid of writing Evil with a capital E lest we should seem out of step with the times. Yet we cannot read the Gospel without being struck by the ubiquity of the Evil One who sets himself against Jesus:

> The clash of wills is constant, even when it is not a prominent feature of the narrative. No sooner does the Saviour begin his public life than Satan plainly reveals his hostility. The story of Jesus' temptation in the wilderness is, as it were, the preface to the mission that the Saviour is about to fulfil and the key to the drama soon to be enacted on Calvary . . . The hostile presence of the Adversary is implicit at every stage of the narrative, and when Jesus yields up his spirit on the cross, the inspired writer notes—not as a point of detail, but because of the event's deep theological implications—that the sky 'grows dark' over Jerusalem.[1]

If Christ conquered death, sin and the Powers of Darkness, it remains for us to make his victory our own, progressively.

2. THE METHOD, FROM THE ANGLE OF INTEGRATION

How can we make the necessary integration of nature with grace a reality in our lives?

The guidance we need on this subject must be provided by a theological anthropology.

The true knowledge of man is given to us by God, in his Word and through the Church, who, as Paul VI used to say, is 'an expert in humanity'. The person's human, psychological and relational formation must be given within his specifically Christian formation, and be enshrined in the latter, not juxtaposed to it. The Christian must welcome Christ from the vantage point of a *unified* vision of man, not a fragmented one. The understanding given to us by faith bears on both the mystery of God and the mystery of man.

When faith weakens and spiritual apathy sets in, our merely human equilibrium deteriorates. Then we search the human sciences for what we can no longer find at the life-giving spring of the Spirit—and with all the attendant risks: inner conflict, linguistic and conceptual ambiguities, the doubtful search for a 'third way' lying between a weakened spiritual investment and a purely naturalistic conception which does not really incorporate the Christian vocation.

It would be disastrous to believe that the formation given in the Church is incapable of ensuring an all-round development of persons, that grace does not have enough scope to evangelize man's psyche, his relationships and desires, and that the solution must be sought elsewhere.

The experience of the Pentecostal Renewal shows clearly that, starting from our baptismal grace and its possible resurgences, God ceaselessly builds and rebuilds persons and communities.

The experience of the Word received in the Spirit shows that this Word of God, endowed with an incomparable power to mobilize and regenerate men, is also capable of setting them on their feet and of giving a new impetus to the most damaged and endangered lives. 'Only say the word and I shall be healed.'

The experience of the Renewal shows plainly that the Church is endowed by the Spirit with a capacity to reach into man's heart, to touch him in his innermost depths and wound, and to heal him through the intimate reconciliation of his being, thus instantly transforming the horizon of his life. Why does the Lord delight in healing him through grace, and in the very roots of his being? Why does he give our time this sign, if not to show his children that he is and remains the Father of Mercy and that Jesus is the Saviour of the whole of man and all mankind?

3. THE METHOD, FROM THE ANGLE OF SACRAMENTAL INTEGRATION

The test of the right pedagogical harmonizing of nature and grace will be the place accorded to the mediation of Christ, led by the Spirit, in the sacramental life of the Christian advancing on his path.

So we would have to examine what role is fulfilled, in man's human and Christian development, by the sacraments, which are the vital channels of the Holy Spirit at work in the Church. To believe in the 'life-giving' Spirit is to believe, concretely, in his vivifying action through the sacraments. If the Church is Jesus Christ, continued in and by the Holy Spirit, its action, which transforms man, is essential. Although in the past we erred on the side of sacramentalism, that is to say, a too routine-like practice of the sacraments, the tendency of our time is to favour communal, paraliturgical celebrations, because of their prayerful, spontaneous and warm atmosphere, but at the risk of blurring the eucharistic celebration itself, or of relegating it to the background.

The attitude we take to each sacrament is therefore an essential test by which to judge whether we are progressing correctly on our Christian path.

The danger I have stressed invites us to ask ourselves a few questions which can serve as tests:

What is the Christian's position in regard to baptism, the Eucharist and the sacrament of penance? Let us confine this brief examination to these three sacraments which are vital to every Christian life.

(a) *Baptism*

How much faith do Christians place today in infant baptism which, as specified both by tradition and the new code of canon law, must be conferred on infants within a few weeks of their birth?

At present there is an increasingly prevalent tendency to defer the child's baptism, so that he may opt for it personally when he is old enough to take such a decision. This practice is indicative of a diminishing faith in the sacramental reality of baptism, which is the starting point of every Christian life.

In a page of *A New Pentecost*? I have attempted to explain why parents should opt for the traditional infant baptism, without letting themselves be seduced by pseudo-liberal arguments:

> Let us establish this, first by reflecting from the point of view of the parents themselves and then, at a deeper level, from the point of view of God who comes to meet the child at this beginning of his life.
>
> If we consider first, the point of view of parental responsibility, we see that, naturally, parents must assume responsibilities on behalf of their children. They have brought the child into the world, and immediately they are faced with making decisions for him as to what is for his good. They want to give him, from the first moment of his life, all their tender care, all their attention, which their own experience has taught them will be beneficial for him, even when this involves making certain decisions without consulting him. Their watchful and unfaltering love surrounds the child constantly. This is the beauty of their love, that they are not waiting for a recompense. Without being aware of it, they are following the way in which God loves us: he first loves us, without awaiting our initiative or gratitude.
>
> Jesus said the same of the Christian vocation: 'You did not choose me, I chose you' (John 15:16). It is a response to this choice, this initial love of God for us. Should we not follow this principle when it comes to baptism? From the

beginning of the child's life God wishes to give the best of himself, his inner life: this is the meaning of baptism. Baptism introduces the child into divine intimacy, joins him to the mystery of the death and resurrection of the Lord himself, opens him to the grace of the Holy Spirit. These are all real riches even if at the beginning the child is unaware of this. It is important that an awareness of these realities should grow slowly, in the process of a Christian life nourished by the Eucharist. To postpone baptism is to deprive the child of this growth of grace within him. It is to take away from the young person, in the name of freedom, what will be, at the moment of a decisive choice, an inestimable treasure that is the experience of living the Christian life. By depriving the child of this experience, he, whether one wishes it or not, is being 'conditioned' and this lacuna will be a powerful factor in his making a choice: he cannot with impunity breathe a rarefied religious atmosphere at home and a hostile atmosphere outside. The liberty of the child is not safeguarded by denying him an experience which can help motivate his free choice at the deepest level.[2]

(b) *The Eucharist*

An analogous question arises concerning the integration of the Eucharist into the life and rhythm of growth of each Christian.

It has been rightly said that the Church 'does' the Eucharist, but that the Eucharist 'makes' the Church. For, as the supreme sacrament, it associates us, literally, with the death and life of Jesus, sweeping us, with him and in him, into a mystery of adoration, gratitude, supplication and forgiveness.

It is also a mystery of Communion in the Lord's Body and Blood which, for our sake, have become our food and drink. The Christian cannot safely manage without their power of life.

Nor should we be doing justice to the breadth and wealth of

this mystery if we did not also prolong it into the intimacy of the silent adoration that recognizes the Lord's Presence in our tabernacles. A Presence that 'flows from the sacrifice and disposes us to sacramental and spiritual Communion', as a papal document so aptly points out.[3]

The depth of our Christian life therefore depends on this vital integration. And not only at the individual level, but also at the level of the whole community. For it is the Eucharist that really integrates the assembly into the Body of Christ. It not only provides a link between the Resurrection and each one of us, but makes us a sharing people whenever we 'share' it. It not only provides the foundation of a social morality, but takes us far beyond social ethics and opens us to an essential conception of human solidarity: it is 'the sacrament of brotherhood'.

(c) *The Sacrament of Reconciliation*

Here too nature and grace must work together. We have a number of techniques to restore man to full psychological health and set him on his feet. And they are commendable, but also, by their very nature, limited techniques. For the Christian, it is the Sacrament of Penance which, surpassing our human wisdom, brings men a renewing and restoring grace.

In a series of talks on Penance (February 1984), John Paul II carefully analysed the various aspects and stages leading to the Lord's regenerating forgiveness in the Sacrament of Reconciliation. Speaking of the examination of conscience which precedes the forgiveness of sins, the Holy Father said:

> The examination of conscience is revealed to us not only as an effort of psychological introspection, or as an intimate act which is restricted to the boundary of our conscience, abandoned to itself. It is above all a confrontation . . . a coming face to face with the Lord Jesus himself, the Son of

> God, who willed to assume our human condition (cf. Phil. 2:7), to take up the burden of our sins (Isa. 53:12) and to conquer them through Death and Resurrection.
>
> Only in the divine light which is revealed in Christ and which lives in the Church can we clearly detect our faults. Only in the presence of the Lord Jesus who offers his life 'for us and for our salvation' shall we succeed in confessing our sins . . . In this way, the sinner not only knows himself as though through induction, but he knows himself by way of reflection: when he sees himself as God himself sees him in the Lord Jesus; when he accepts himself because God himself in the Lord Jesus accepts him and makes him a 'new creation' (Gal. 6:15). The divine 'judgement' is revealed for what it is: a freely given pardon.[4]

The Pope then discusses other aspects of the Sacrament of Penance, such as the natural and supernatural benefits inherent in the confession of sins, a confession that liberates the penitent.

This vision of faith invites the Christian in search of his 'I' to let the Lord himself enlighten him about it, to let himself be guided and saved from himself by the grace of confession and sacramental forgiveness. Then he will discover by experience that this sacramental renewal of the self works in him, mysteriously, as a kind of transfusion of the Redeemer's precious blood, acting in him as an inestimable life force, a 'spiritual booster' which he needs for his journey through life.

1. L. J. Suenens, *Renewal and the Powers of Darkness* (London, Darton, Longman and Todd, 1983), p. 8.

2. L. J. Suenens, *A New Pentecost?* (New York, Seabury Press, 1975), pp. 125–6.
3. Introduction to *Inestimabile Donum*, no. 20, 1980.
4. *The Pope Teaches* (London, CTS, March 1984), pp. 82–4.

X

Methods of Growth, in Psychological Analysis

1. THE RESPECTIVE ROLES OF THE PRIEST AND THE LAYMAN AS GUIDES

Every method of self-analysis forms part of a broader and more comprehensive formation. In dealing with the growth of Christian individuals and communities, we cannot separate the human formation from the spiritual formation, for they are intimately united.

This inevitably raises the question of the relation between the priest and the layman acting as guides and counsellors. Although, in some cases, the layman can act as a spiritual director, only the priest may hear confession: these two domains must remain separate and distinct.

There is a danger of overemphasizing the role of the priest and of drifting into clericalism. On the other hand, there is the equally unwelcome possibility that the lay guide may assume a role for which he is not qualified, or claim that his inspiration comes directly from the Lord. At the moment, and generally speaking, I do not fear that the priest is excessively authoritarian. Rather I would suggest that he is too self-effacing and that he is sometimes disconcerted or moved by the fervour which he observes around him, and from which he himself benefits.

A consequence of the present situation is that there are communities in which the priest does not play his specific role. Yet, thanks to his training and the many years he has devoted to the study of philosophy and theology, he is normally well equipped to give the requisite spiritual and doctrinal guidance when he is called upon to 'discern' (a word that recurs again and again) how he should proceed, particularly in regard to the authentication of extraordinary charisms. His task is to maintain the balance between nature and grace, and to guide along safe paths the members of a community desiring to be religious and apostolic.

Sometimes the priest is simply a member of the group, in no way different from the other members; he does not even sit on the council which determines the community's future action and takes major decisions regarding its religious life and work. This is particularly true of communities which have not yet drawn up a Constitution recognized by the Church, or depend, in the final reckoning, only on the group's founder or animator. The priest works with the other members in a 'brotherly' situation, but the 'paternal' dimension is absent, which is not normal.

St Augustine used to say to his flock in Hippo: 'For you I am a bishop, with you I am a Christian.' The priest should be recognized both as a pastor mandated by his bishop and as a brother among brothers.

All this in no way prevents the layman from acting, very legitimately, as a spiritual guide. Eastern Orthodoxy has for centuries been well acquainted with the figure of the *staretz*, a lay monk who attracts pilgrims eager to benefit from his spiritual gifts. We all know lay people—men and women—whose depth of spiritual life inspires and enriches everyone around them. So there is room here for an osmosis, a mutually enriching spiritual exchange.

When there is a divergence of views involving the doctrinal

and spiritual plane, it is normally incumbent on the priest to use his own discernment, as the first step, and if the problem proves complex, to refer it to the authority that has mandated him: his bishop.

Down the centuries, the credibility of saints who were not priests (I am thinking here of Francis of Assisi, who was only a deacon, and of St Ignatius, who was ordained late in life) has owed much to their readiness to seek the advice of their bishop or Rome, in order to authenticate their mission.

Generally speaking, such a step may involve personal suffering, for even saints remain human, but it is implicit in our faith in 'the one apostolic Church', which recognizes its bishops as the successors of the apostles. And it devolves on the bishop to guide his flock and to discern the charisms of the Spirit.

2. INTROSPECTION IS NOT SELF-ABSORPTION

It is quite legitimate for a person to take his own growth 'in hand', provided that he does not succumb to narcissism and bears in mind the Lord's saying that no one, for all his virtues, can add one cubit to his stature. We cannot watch ourselves growing, and introspection carried out in lengthy sessions and analyses is not only a very uncertain way of knowing oneself, but can foster many illusions.

Moreover, the method is too expensive to be available to everyone: this in itself is an indication that the normal paths of self-development should be more simple, less exclusive and within everyone's reach.

By all means let us examine ourselves, but provided that it does not become an obsession, or an expensive pastime, or an occasion for self-absorption, to the detriment of our calling to devote ourselves to all the spiritual and material troubles of a world in distress.

We have countless ways of learning to know ourselves: for example, through friends sincere enough to tell us the truth about ourselves. And also by paying heed to criticisms, even when they are unkind. The ancient adage *Fas est ab hoste doceri* (it is right to be taught even by an enemy) remains valid even in psychology. The directors of large companies are often prepared to pay high fees to consultants who study their management problems on the spot and point out mistakes and defects (including those of the boss). This is sound realism and a wise investment!

3. THE RELATIVITY OF EACH METHOD

The judgement we make on a given method will also largely depend on the way the method describes itself. If it claims to be a self-sufficient method from which 'even God can benefit', instead of more modestly presenting itself as one approach among others (introspection, for example, is just one of several paths to self-knowledge), there is good reason to fear that it is overestimating its worth.

True science acknowledges the relativity of its frame of reference. Even in this sphere, humility plays a constructive role, and no scientist can safely do without it.

One feels very wary of a method which claims to be universal, and states that it 'serves an intuition on the emergence and growth of Man within man, and on the emergence of the Human Society from the midst of today's societies'. Even the capital letters are ambiguous.

This kind of exaggeration is an ever-recurring temptation when Science (with a capital) is transformed into scientism, psychology into psychologism, and they unwittingly become pseudo-religions or pseudo-mystiques.

4. THE GUIDES

The requisite psychological competence should be determined according to the normal rules of professional qualification. In every sphere of study, there are laws governing the conferring of diplomas according to recognized, objective and scientific criteria.

The fact of having followed a certain number of courses is not a sufficient guarantee that a person is qualified to direct courses in his turn. One is entitled to demand that his performance be judged by a board of examiners, according to objective norms and rigorous criteria.

Moreover, the guide himself should not be a person with problems, labouring under mental distress or a sense of injury.

But if we wish to apply a sound Christian method, it is further advisable to take account of all the points I made earlier on the necessity of harmoniously combining nature with grace. This presupposes that the guide has a religious qualification, guaranteed, in this case too, by the competent ecclesial authority.

5. THE GUIDED

The guided, too, must take precautions. It has been wisely said that no method can work unless its followers are free of serious problems pertaining to their personal equilibrium. But who checks and supervises this 'customs clearance' before the students begin the course?

How can one discern the saturation point and prevent

students who, in the early stages of the course, feel that they are benefiting from it, from becoming, so to speak, intoxicated by the method because it has been unduly prolonged?

To be valid, a method has to be practised in valid circumstances. It is quite usual for a prospectus to state that the method is not suitable for people with problems—whether personal, social, or stemming from depression, psychological instability, the breakdown of a marriage, and so on. The real issue is: who selects the candidates and according to what criteria? Or is the course, in fact, available to all and sundry? The same applies to the creation of groups. Inevitably, the group's sharing will be conditioned by persons brought together by chance, and this chance factor will create further problems. It is most advisable and necessary to select the candidates carefully from the start and before embarking on the method.

Let us also bear in mind that if, in theory, each participant in the session is told that he is free to decide whether or not he will share his personal problems and experiences with the group, in practice the atmosphere is conducive to the unburdening of confidences, to an openness which may be unwise, especially when there is a very mixed assortment of participants.

Lastly, once the method is applied, how can we safeguard the psychological freedom of those men and women who submit themselves to it, and avoid such dangers as infantilism, growing dependence, brain-washing, in short the illusion of freedom subtly manipulated by the guide's unconscious ascendancy over the guided?

The value of a method must be judged according to the degree of emancipation which it engenders, even in regard to the method itself. 'He must increase, but I must decrease', said John the Baptist, the forerunner of Jesus. Every educator and instructor should regard this saying as the test of the validity of his method. 'Set your child down on the pavement and teach him to walk confidently without your support', advised Montaigne. An introspective method must be rigorously tested in the light of this criterion. Does it create dependence, psychological servitude? Or does it foster freedom, a blossoming of the personality, a sense of personal responsibility in that pupil who is following the method as a temporary measure, and precisely so that he may learn to manage without it in time?

6. HOW DO YOU JUDGE A TREE BY ITS FRUIT?

There are apparently excellent fruits, doubtful fruits and bad fruits. There are also immediate but perishable fruits. Some fruits ripen overnight, while others need more time.

There are fruits that may be good for a particular individual, but harmful collectively. There are fruits that may be good at a certain level, yet become harmful through omission because, among other things, they highlight only one aspect of a much wider truth. When we are dealing with the person's human and Christian formation, the care we devote to his full equilibrium and the coordination of partial, complementary aspects can never be too great.

If the person submitting himself to a particular method of psychological therapy is well balanced and has already received a solid religious and spiritual formation, he can benefit from the method for a limited period because, in these favourable circumstances, it is assimilated by a complete personality that relativizes it, supplies the omissions and tones down the exaggerations. The tree's fruit must be determined in relation to the abundant sap that already circulates through it and nourishes it.

So in order to judge a method objectively, we must take account of the questionable or harmful fruits it bears for all its 'clients', including those with no previous formation and for whom the most harmful effects may well be excessive psychological dependence, narcissism and naturalistic self-sufficiency. These are very real dangers.

XI

At the Meeting-Point of Nature and Grace

1. THE CHRISTIAN, A SOCIAL BEING

In the previous pages I have attempted to stress the necessity of harmoniously integrating nature with grace in the growth of the human being. I would like to conclude this study by underlining the Christian's social dimension and some of its pastoral implications at the convergence and meeting-point of nature and grace.

Although we all acknowledge that man is a social being, in relationship with others, we have not sufficiently elicited the consequences of this fact regarding his total formation and his behaviour as a 'collective' rather than individual Christian. We are gradually emerging from an age of individualism when the inmost self was reserved and would open itself to others only half-heartedly and superficially. In such a climate men live side by side and coexist, but there is little true fellowship between them.

On the plane of lived Christianity, we still have a long way to go before we emerge from this state of coexistence, of inhibitions and complexes, which so often make relationships artificial and superficial. In my view, the key to the future of any in-depth Christian renewal lies in the expressions 'sharing' and 'living in true fellowship' with each other.

The Christian is a being 'in fellowship' with others. He is

invited to say the *Our Father* with a stress on the plural and to translate the requirements of his faith in terms of brotherhood. For the idolatrous and hypertrophic cult of self he must substitute a sense of 'we', both when he speaks to God and when he stretches out his hand to his brother. The Lord makes the eucharistic rendezvous with the Christian, and requires him to keep it, precisely because it is the supreme mystery of communion with him, and with others in him.

It is towards this ideal that the Christian of the new age must strain, if he wishes to live his faith in a completely logical way. It is by losing himself in the mystery of the mystical Body that he will find his Christian stature and the full blossoming of the purpose for which he was created.

A Christian cannot live his faith as a solitary being. He needs to live it with other Christians who quite literally 'share' it with him. And all Christians must share their faith with each other, in mutually enriching exchanges. *Vae soli*: 'It is not good that man should live alone', says God at the beginning of Genesis (2:18) when he creates Eve as a companion for Adam.

If man is a social being, the Christian is doubly so: by reason of his creation, and by reason of his baptism, which incorporates him into one Body and makes him an integral part of it.

What is an ontological reality must become a psychological reality.

'Even the Pope needs brothers', wrote Patriarch Athenagoras. He needs them for his own equilibrium, and for his human and supernatural growth. This law of sharing is vital to all Christians, and at all times, but especially in our time when the sociological supports of a Christian society have practically disappeared, and all values are called into question, while religion itself is being privatized and isolated from public life.

The success of the Rogerian 'sensitivity groups', with all their attendant ambiguities, due to various factors such as psychological unblocking with no safeguards, warns us that, deep in man's heart, there is a need for sharing and communication.

In this respect, the present proliferation of sects, many of whose members are disillusioned Christians who have left the Church, deserves to be studied closely: it is a warning which must urge us to examine our own conscience.

There is no denying that the popularity of today's sects is partly due to the fact that their followers feel really integrated into an intimate group where each person is acknowledged, called by his name, and has close ties with the other members. This shows that every person has a heartfelt longing to belong to a community: this need can be translated and expressed in a wide variety of ways, but the fact itself is a sign that we cannot afford to disregard, especially in our pastoral work.

I cannot but hope that a Christian pedagogy in which nature and grace are harmoniously united will succeed in evaluating and incorporating the findings of the human sciences with a view to a better understanding of man and interhuman relations. We would all be much enriched if the various methods of analysis, self-discovery and mutual openness were to combine their conclusions on 'man-in-relationship' into a Christian vision. This would also be a victory over individualism which still holds the lives of far too many Christians in its vice-like grip.

Although the present proliferation of sects is a warning to us, the birth of numerous Christian communities of a new type, for which the code of canon law has not yet made provisions, is a very hopeful sign, provided that there, too, the necessary balance is maintained.

It is not desirable to organize the formation given in a Christian community in such a way that there is a *discrepancy* between its human-relational aspect and its theological-spiritual aspect.

The entire formation of a baptized person, especially if he is called to devote his intimate life to the service of the Kingdom, must be given in the light of divine Revelation and the Word of God. Every science and knowledge of man must take God as its starting-point and develop from there. For man receives his life from God, and his life is the glory of God.

If the vision of man and the world, particularly in youth education, is not a *well-integrated* vision, starting from Revelation, every subsequent educational approach—whether psychological, moral or religious—risks being flawed by that initial imbalance. And the very language used in such a formation risks reflecting a fundamental ambiguity.

One of the reasons for this initial difficulty may well be that, whereas the Christian vision of man and the world proceeds by *inclusion*, the vision of the human sciences operates by *reduction*. When they are juxtaposed in education, these two different approaches may result in a confusion of viewpoints and values.

The Christian vision of the human being, created in the likeness of God, does not in any sense disregard the importance of numerous factors (biological, psycho-sociological, etc.) which can explain and determine individual and collective behaviour. The ability to com-prehend and integrate the biblical vision extends to all the reality lived by man.

By contrast, the human sciences do not proceed by inclusion, but by reduction. Their experimental interpretation of the human phenomenon is obliged, by reason of its scientific way of proceeding, to exclude man's transcendental dimension from its field of investigation.

If an experience of a religious nature is recorded, science takes it into account, but as a phenomenon in no way different from any other activity of the mind. The sciences are neither able nor willing to say whether the religious content of the experience is real or imagined. What matters for them is the individual's experience as such, and not the objective or imaginary existence of his points of reference.

Although this way of proceeding is wholly legitimate and consonant with the nature of scientific research, it nevertheless engenders a mentality that easily becomes exclusive.

Since the human sciences as such describe how religion functions for individuals and groups, and reveal the conscious and unconscious components of man's religious desire and its manifestations, they are obliged to consider these phenomena as no more than an experience of the 'I'. And because this approach to man is reductionist from the start, religious realities in general are inevitably regarded as the composite material for a building up of the self by the self, with no other final goal than the fulfilment of the ego and its desire.

But the task of true spiritual discernment is to integrate the global reality of man. At the meeting-point of nature and grace, the Christian life must be discerned, in one glance, as a fully human and fully God-centred life: in short, a life received from God.

2. THE FAMILY AS THE ESSENTIAL NUCLEUS OF COMMUNITY

If individualism is a threat to Christian vitality, it is an even more radical threat to family life and its survival.

It has been said again and again that the family is the social cell *par excellence*. And this is true. But it is precisely at that essential point that we are witnessing an initial and radical tearing of the social fabric. The family is threatened in all its aspects, shaken in its very foundation and centre: the faithful and fruitful conjugal union, based on genuine mutual love, which also implies selflessness and self-control.[1]

We are living in a climate of moral vagary dominated by individualism. An isolated Christian family, confronted with all the Powers of Evil at work, needs to stand together with other Christian families, in order to fulfil the requirements of its faith and life. The Lord said that 'where two or three are gathered in his Name, He would be among them'. This promise also holds true for two or three families gathered to live their Christian life together. Besides, a husband and wife are not a duality but a unity, and the gospel text can be applied, even as a mathematical proposition, to several families gathered in his Name to pursue the same quest.

In alluding to the Spirit of Evil who destroys the unity of marriage and the family, it is by no means my intention to overlook the considerable advances our time has made towards a better understanding of Love and its components. Very fortunately, we have got away from the excesses of Jansenism, but in reacting against them, we have all too often lost sight of the values we have to preserve and apply to the needs of our time. Moreover, a specific feature of the Powers of Darkness is that they love to upset the balance of things, to disrupt and destabilize. Everything that helps them to achieve this aim is a fertile soil for their destructive work.

From this standpoint I recommend Cardinal Danneels' magnificent commentary on the *Our Father*, written on thc occasion of the Pope's visit to Belgium. He comments on the last verse, 'Deliver us from evil', as follows:

> Evil has many faces, O Lord,
> and surrounds us on all sides:
> Individual and collective egoism, self-interest, divisions, violence in hearts and structures, the absence of rules in a world adrift.
>
> This evil, which also dwells in our hearts, is not a blind force, but a refined, intelligent and scheming power; it is the prince of darkness, the Evil One who, from the very begin-

ning, has sown discord in hearts, homes and entire continents. Father, deliver us from the Evil One.

3. LED BY THE HOLY SPIRIT

If the Christian is to conduct a valid self-exploration, he must be guided by good psychology. But for his undertaking to succeed, a minimum of theology, or simply of faith, remains essential and vital. In the light of Jesus Christ dwelling in us, he will discover himself and, in addition, he will understand the meaning of renunciation, obedience, faithfulness to life—and the meaning of a few other virtues which can have no significance if Christ is not the Way, the Truth and the Life of man. These consequences are far-reaching.

Let me repeat this: when we are charting paths of spiritual growth for the Christian, we have to make a careful distinction between what pertains to psychology and what belongs to the sphere of his Christian faith. An approach aiming to deepen the inner life cannot be equated with the path of spiritual growth. In a discussion between Father Varillon, S.J., and Marcel Legaut, published under the title *Two Christians on the Way*, Father Varillon asked Marcel Legaut not to use terms like 'interiority' and 'spirituality', or 'inner life' and 'spiritual life' as if they were practically synonymous:

> I believe that much confusion would be avoided if we defined our terms: the inner life is life with oneself, reflection, meditation, a deeper understanding of the human self such as even an atheist can pursue. Jean Rostand, for example, had an inner life because he sincerely worshipped truth; a great love implies an inner life.
>
> But the innermost self is not God. God is an Other, the Wholly Other. The spiritual life is life with that Other, the Holy Spirit, in the light of the Holy Spirit, *in Spiritu Sancto*.

> The innermost centre of my inner life is the Holy Spirit. Within me he is 'more myself than I am'.

This distinction is of vital importance.

I would like to invite the Christian reader to set every attempt at introspection and personal growth in the light of the Holy Spirit.

At Pentecost the Church's liturgy places on our lips a prayer that entreats the Holy Spirit to come down on us with his transfiguring power:

> Wash thou what is stained,
> Water what is dry,
> Heal thou what is wounded,
> Bend thou what is stiff,
> Warm thou what is chill,
> Guide thou what has strayed.

A humble and magnificent prayer, full of hope, for it carries us beyond ourselves and leads us to our final blossoming in God's heart.

4. A SYMBOL

As I wrote the title of this last chapter, *At the Meeting-Point of Nature and Grace*, I was suddenly visited by a memory. A memory of one of the most peaceful and moving beauty spots I know in Ireland. It is a tourist haunt which, at first sight, looks like a lake because it is so still. In reality it lies at the confluence of two rivers whose waters mingle and interflow so deeply that they seem motionless. The place is called 'the Meeting of the Waters'.

This image is an eloquent symbol. In its own way, it translates what I have tried to express throughout this book: by the will of God, nature and grace are one in us, and in our personal formation we can never separate what God has united: the human and the divine in man. It is there that full human development and the glory of God come together. And there lies the message and all the hope of these pages.

1. L. J. Suenens, *Love and Control* (London, Burns and Oates, 1961).